the
freelance
academic

transform your creative life and career

THE FREELANCE ACADEMIC

Transform Your Creative Life and Career

KATIE ROSE GUEST PRYAL

Blue Crow Books

Publisher's Cataloging-in-Publication Data
Pryal, Katie Rose Guest. 1976-.
The Freelance Academic: Transform Your Creative Life and Career / Katie Rose
Guest Pryal
p.____ cm.____
ISBN 978-1-947834-35-4 (Pbk.) | 978-1-947834-36-1 (Ebook)
1. Education, Higher. 2. College Teachers. 3. Autobiography. I. Title.
814'.6 | PCN 2019901252

Published by Blue Crow Books
an imprint of Blue Crow Publishing, LLC
Chapel Hill, NC
www.bluecrowpublishing.com
Cover Design by Lauren Faulkenberry

Also by Katie Rose Guest Pryal

FICTION

Entanglement

Love and Entropy

Chasing Chaos

How to Stay

Fallout Girl

Take Your Charming Somewhere Else

NONFICTION

Life of the Mind Interrupted: Essays on Mental Health and Disability in Higher Education

We Are All Enemies of the State: And Other Essays on Speech

Even If You're Broken: Essays on Sexual Assault and #MeToo

The Freelance Academic: Transform Your Creative Life and Career

Praise for LIFE OF THE MIND INTERRUPTED

The advice and practical information makes this book a must read, not just for those in academia.

New York Times Bestselling author Kate Moretti for *Booktrib*

Pryal is one of the foremost writers of disability and higher education we have today.

Catherine Prendergast, Ph.D., author of *Buying into English: Language and Investment in the New Capitalist World*

This is not a book to miss.

Kelly J. Baker, Ph.D., award-winning author of *Sexism Ed: Essays on Gender and Labor in Higher Education*

These thoughtfully chosen and arranged essays grapple with issues relevant to disabled students and scholars as well as those who would be allies.

Kecia Ali, Ph.D., author of *Sexual Ethics and Islam: Feminist Reflections on Qur'an, Hadith, and Jurisprudence*

Praise for THE FREELANCE ACADEMIC

A roadmap that's as practical as it is hopeful.

Bestselling author Camille Pagán for *Booktrib Magazine*

Both a cautionary tale and a beacon of hope.

Foreword Reviews

So many academics—current, former, and struggling—will see themselves in Pryal's story. I hope just as many see all of the possibilities she enumerates, and understand, as she does, that the passions and talents that draw us to the university in the first place are often best used outside it.

Rebecca Schuman, Ph.D., author of *Schadenfreude, A Love Story*

With candor and vulnerability, Pryal shares her own experiences and hard-fought wisdom to make a compelling case for a rewarding professional life beyond the walls of traditional academia.

Amy Impellizzeri, award-winning novelist and author of *Lawyer Interrupted: Successfully Transitioning from the Practice of Law—and Back Again*

A new, necessary book.

Catherine J. Prendergast, Ph.D., author of *Buying into English: Language and Investment in the New Capitalist World*

For Michael, who helped me take the leap.
For my boys, who remind me what I'm working for.

Contents

Foreword

I am a freelance academic. And I have been for at least six years. I left my academic post, as a lecturer, in 2013, and I had no idea what I was going to do with my career or my life even. I floundered and flailed as I tried to figure out what I wanted to be when I grew up, except I was already a grown-up with two kids in tow and no idea how to shift to a career that wasn't an academic one. So, I started freelance writing, built on my academic work to become a (paid) public speaker, worked as a higher ed journalist, tried a lot of things that never panned out, and finally realized I had a talent for editing. (Who would have guessed that grading hundreds of undergraduate papers a semester would build my editing skills?)

I became a freelance academic, but the problem was I didn't know it. I described my career as "adjacent to academia," which explained how I positioned myself but not really what my career was. I didn't have the vocabulary to describe what my new career —outside the academy—fully entailed. I moved from graduate student to adjunct to full-time lecturer to part-time writer and stay-at-home mom. Then, I added gigs that included editing a magazine on higher education, writing nonfiction books that weren't academic monographs, developmental editing books for academics and memoirist. I dread pulling together a bio because there's not an elegant way to capture all the types of gigs that I do each year. I patch-worked a career, which appears more catch-all than consistent.

When I give the short version of what I do, I explain that I'm an editor, writer, and speaker with a religious Studies PhD. Try putting all of those on a business card or say them five times really fast. Instead, I have two business cards: one for my main gig as editor of *Women in Higher Education* and one for everything else. Somewhere in my office, the front room of my house really, there's a box with old business cards with a different title from my time in the ivory tower. Artifacts of the life I thought I would lead that never quite worked out.

I trained to be an academic. I ended up being something else entirely. It's taken me years to realize that I'm not alone. And you won't be either if you decide to step outside the academy and build a different career, a different life. Katie is here to help you, as she's helped me as a colleague and friend, to realize that it's okay to create your own career and show you how. It was more than okay to build a career that I wanted rather than the one everyone expected me to have. Just because I trained to be a scholar didn't mean I had to be one. I had more agency than I knew. I could and did master new skills. I could rely on what I learned in my PhD to do something different, terrifying and new. I could create a legacy to be proud of. I could do all those things if I just decided to.

You can do all those things too. You can be a freelance academic too, if you let Katie lead the way. And you should let her lead the way.

If you are picking up this book right now, you are already considering options beyond academic careers. (It's good to see what's out there.) Or maybe, you just want to see what the possibilities for your career might be. (Another good choice.) Or maybe, you just want a swift kick in the pants to convince you to make a change. (Which can also be good.)

I'm happy to tell you, dear reader, that this book offers you all three.

Katie provides the how-tos of building your career as a freelance academic, explains the labor exploitation endemic to higher ed, and tells you what worked and what didn't for her.

One of the things I tend to hate, and I do mean hate, about these typical stories of transitions is that they are easy exit and entry stories. The person quits their academic post and then lands a new job, almost instantly. They are out of one career and then into another. Everything seems so damn easy. Nothing is bumpy, frustrating, or taxing. A can-do attitude is all you need. It's not though.

Part of the reason for my strong feelings about easy, frictionless stories is that they were antithetical to what I experienced. There was instant success. And here I was trudging and toiling with some wins but mostly I had a stack of rejections or, even worse, the radio silence that suggested I wasn't even worth responding to. If a résumé or pitch goes out into the world and no one responds, did you actually send it?

It was hard not to feel like a failure when all the advice suggested anyone could make the shift from academic work to alternative academic work. And yet, I wasn't a failure; those career transitions are hard. They take hard work, luck, energy, and time. Things often don't pan out, but sometimes, they do.

Katie's honesty about her own journey, then, is rare among the stories of transitions out of higher ed. You get to learn from her mistakes because she's brave enough to share them. You get the benefit of hard-learned lessons as well as realizing that failure teaches something important and is unavoidable. Learning from what doesn't work show us what does. Her advice is golden as she prods you to really think about the career you want and what it takes to make that happen.

As I was reading *The Freelance Academic*, I wished that I had had this book six years ago, so I would have felt like I could have pulled together a career outside of academia with a lot less anguish, sleepless nights, and utter terror.

So, reader, sit down and get comfy and be ready to take notes. This book is like a good coffee date with that friend who is kind (and maybe a little bit bossy). She's the friend that wants what is best for you, and she's determined to make that happen. She's guiding (maybe, prodding?) you to have the career and life you want. She's laying down the options and how to make them happen. Let Katie be that friend. Let her guide and advise you. Listen to what she has to say. And then, take the plunge. Build that career you want. Become a freelance academic. And never look back.

Kelly J. Baker
January 2019

Prologue: A Lecturer's Almanac

March 2007

THE HALL OF THE DEPARTMENT IS A 1960s-ERA BUNKER, MOLDED OF concrete and rebar, with tall, narrow windows to repel even the most determined activist. I watch my feet as I climb the linoleum-clad stairs so I don't stumble in my skinny high heels, bought specifically to match this suit. The suit is black, with pale pinstripes, more fashionable than the interview suit.

After the years I'd spent working as a lawyer, I'd always sworn I would never buy one of those.

Dr. Composition and Dr. Rhetoric sit in a conference room. He's tenured and directs the first-year writing program; she's an assistant professor. I have a new doctorate in rhetoric and composition, the "most marketable" degree as everyone on my dissertation committee promised me. And it seems so, since Dr. Composition and Dr. Rhetoric want to hire me for this special position, crafted just for me or someone like me, for someone with special training in special disciplines, like law.

Plus, Dr. Composition says, it pays really well and comes with great research support. Sure it's still a contract position, but the contract is multi-year, and the Department Chair is really committed to changing the lecturer paradigm.

Dr. Composition says, when I ask about the possibility for contract renewal, "I promise we'll continue to exploit you as long as you let us."

Dr. Composition laughs at his joke. I smile to show I'm hip to the humor, but really, I don't understand what's so funny. Dr. Rhetoric looks uncomfortable, but she smiles in the way that women do when they know they must to keep the peace.

April 2007

I moved here for him, for Mr. Tall. Like many women before me, I traded some super-bright job offers for a pretty darn shiny one and a bungalow with the man I love.

In late April, I get a phone call from the chair of an English department in a city many states away. He's calling to offer me a position at his school, one I applied for months ago. I say I've taken a job at the Bunker, so I'm not available anymore.

He says, "I'm not surprised. Talent like yours gets snatched up quick."

When I hear his words, I feel a twinge, thinking maybe I've accepted a job that isn't good enough, that I should have held out for something better.

But I convince myself I'm satisfied. The job is a good one. Only six courses a year—a great course load for a lecturer. And the pay, it's not so bad. And isn't it more important to be near the person I care about most in the world? Would I really trade Mr. Tall for the tenure-track?

A few days later, Mr. Tall says he wants to take me to dinner near the Bunker. First, he suggests a walk around campus. He says, "I've always loved this place at dusk."

A decade ago, my new institution belonged to him, a skinny kid with big round glasses who came on a full scholarship. The coincidence across space and time suits my love of scientific anomalies. We stop outside my Bunker-to-be, and he pulls me into the foyer. We stop at the Board, with its black background and white letters, the long list of professors' last names with digits adjacent indicating the small rooms where genius happens.

"Your name will be up there soon," he says.

Outside, in the warm spring evening, he drops to a knee, holding something round and shiny. "Now you'll think of me every day when you come to work."

August 2007

The syllabi are written. The readings selected and scanned. The bus schedule memorized. The office keys placed on my keychain, the copy codes in my head. I am, I believe, ready.

My office, I discover, was painted pink and yellow, each wall a solid pane of color, by the graduate students who inhabited it before me. Pink paint splatters the ceiling and the baseboards, yellow drips have dried on the desks and linoleum. I hang my four diplomas, hoping to distract visitors from the unprofessional colors with my professional credentials.

I visit Dr. Rhetoric's office, professionally painted a refreshing spring green. She reassures me that the department pays to repaint offices. "You just have to ask," she says.

A few days later, I request a repainting. I learn that, because I am a lecturer, the department will not pay to repaint my office.

Every time a student comes for office hours, there's a funny moment when the shocking colors evoke an unintentional response, often pursed lips, or a sniff as though the colors emit a smell. Embarrassed, I lie, "The walls will be repainted soon. Don't worry."

I learn my office is to be shared. My office-mate is also a lecturer, one of the special lecturers like me, hired as part of the new model for fixed-term faculty. Each week, she travels far from home to teach here, so she sits in the office a lot, lacking anywhere else to go.

I decide I prefer the campus coffee shop for my office hours. And I buy a new desk for the spare bedroom in the bungalow to have a place to do my writing.

September 2007

They've repainted the hallways of the Bunker. The Bunker's windows don't open, so there's no fresh air. Near the mailboxes, I feel a bit lightheaded from the fumes. Dr. Cultural Studies stands next to me, fumbling with his mail, the same mail I've received, a tightly-packed parcel of fliers, notices, and newsletters, each printed on a different shade of pastel paper.

We stand, our rainbows in our hands, and I say, "The paint smell sure is strong, don't you think?"

He says, without a sign of recognition in his eyes, "You should just be glad they painted." Then he turns and drops his rainbow in the trash.

I wonder if he talks to all faculty that way, or just the young ones, or just the women, or just the ones he doesn't know.

October 2007

I stand in the foyer of the Bunker, where Mr. Tall proposed to me, staring at the Board with its small white letters. My name still isn't there.

———

[one year passes]

———

October 2008

My name does not belong on the Board, I'm told, because lecturers are itinerant, and because to purchase more small, white letters would cost the department too much money.

November 2008

I'm going to have a baby in June.

I hide in the bathroom when I feel sick, armed with a slick pack of lies: I sure gained the newly-wed fifteen, or, Avoid the sushi in the Union today. It's a little off.

December 2008

Faculty meeting. A new course scheduling policy. Each school year, all faculty must teach one semester of Monday, Wednesday, and Friday courses, no exceptions. Many groans emit.

Then, Dr. Twentieth Century says, her voice high and southern and sweet, "I don't see why we can't just have those lecturers teach three days a week. After all, they don't have to write. It's us researchers that should have the good schedules."

I remember some words my mother once said to me when I was in college. She said, "You grow up to be a doctor, do you hear me? Don't you grow up to be a nurse." At the time, I'd just declared an English major, so her words seemed a little strange.

Now I know what she meant. She's been married to a doctor for thirty years, running the practice for twenty. But to some, she'll always be just a doctor's wife.

I became a doctor. But I'm still a nurse. Except nurses get paid more and have better job security.

January 2009

My textbook proposal is accepted by a publisher. I sign my contract at a bistro with Mr. Tall, and he takes my picture with the pen in my hand.

The English Department lecturers form an advisory committee and ask for promotion procedures. We want a senior title, with senior pay, and five year contracts. We form a listserv, start a newsletter with meeting minutes, and begin to plan.

Our push seems to be working.

Meanwhile, to make more money for when the baby comes, I take on an extra course teaching writing at a law school in another city, driving fifty miles each way to get there. The extra course seems like a sensible decision. I never thought I'd be a freeway flier to make ends meet, but I'm happy to have the work.

February 2009

My belly is starting to show, and I'm worried. In addition to English, I also majored in Women's Studies, so I can recognize my fear as an old one. My fear is one working women have felt for decades—that my boss will resent my pregnancy, the promised leave from work (right there in contractual black and white), and the distraction that a child brings.

I've made friends with another lecturer, Dr. Cool. She's been in the Bunker for sixteen years. I stop by her office one afternoon, nervous, needing someone to talk to. She invites me to sit in her office. It's hers alone, and it's bright, with pictures of her grown children on the walls. There are also pictures of Dr. Cool with famous writers she's worked with, like Joan Didion.

"Is your name on the Board?" I ask her.

"No," she says, "and it really makes me mad."

I tell her I'm pregnant. It seems she already knows. She says, "Honey, you should tell everybody. Then they sure as heck can't fire you."

I tell everyone.

I tell our new department chair. She reassures me that not only will I have a job when I get back from parental leave, but that she'll do all in her power to make it as good a job as she can. She tells me she is happy for me, and I believe her.

I sign a form that gives me a semester's paid leave in the fall, and at that moment, I'm really happy that I work in the Bunker.

March 2009

An announcement to all lecturers: Due to budget shortfalls, all lecturers will be placed on one-year contracts for the foreseeable future.

We are reassured, however, that the department—the tenured faculty—will do all it can to protect us.

April 2009

All faculty receive a golden-yellow announcement in the mail, asking for proposals for University-funded small research grants, given to the most promising research projects proposed by any faculty member.

In boldface, like a black eye, the form letter says, Adjunct professors are not eligible, nor are lecturers, instructors, or others of non-professorial rank.

I wonder, if the grants are truly based on merit, why they choose to exclude certain members of the faculty.

I think of high school, when I was a young player on the junior varsity volleyball team. During a preseason scrimmage against the varsity squad, we kicked their butts. Our ever-pragmatic coach simply admitted his error and traded squads, placing the J.V. players on varsity and benching his former starters. Ignoring their protests, he told them, You just need to play better, folks.

I'm starting to wonder about the meaning of merit in the Bunker.

May 2009

My son is born six weeks early.

His skinny, premature form lies in a plastic bin, wires tracking to machines that blip and flash. He eats through a tube. He's weighed every hour. He sleeps under heat lamps and the special UV lamps for jaundice. There are no windows in the nursery. I never know what time of day it is.

For one week he sleeps in that bin, and I forget the Bunker, the Board, the pink-and-yellow office, Dr. Cultural Studies and his disregard, Dr. Twentieth Century and her naïve insults. I think, *If my baby comes home to me safe, nothing else will ever matter again.*

I sit by his bin and grade final papers for my four writing courses. Grades are due in two days.

September 2009

Home with my son, enjoying generous parental leave, I feel like a hypocrite. Sure, no one dreams of growing up to be second-class. But, I tell myself, second-class academia is better than most jobs.

The state budget is getting ugly. Our new chair comes to a lecturers' meeting, where we're finalizing our proposal for the creation of a senior lecturer position. She says, "The budget has been deeply cut. It's not certain that you will all be rehired next year."

Suddenly, the promotion and retention proposal we've been debating, revising, and debating seems pointless.

After the Chair has left, one lecturer says, "We sure got put back in our places. The lecturers were getting uppity."

I go home and say to Mr. Tall, "We're playing *Survivor*. I'm going to lose."

December 2009

In the last faculty meeting of the calendar year, the Senior Lecturer promotion proposal comes up for a vote. Due to budgetary constraints, the bits in the proposal about higher pay and longer contracts are excised. After six years of teaching, a lecturer can put in for a promotion to Senior Lecturer. At least the title will be better.

At the faculty meeting, I point out what appears to be a mistake in the paperwork. It says that all tenure-track faculty can vote on lecturers being promoted to senior lecturer. I think, a first-year assistant professor, who hasn't even passed third-year review, shouldn't be able to vote on a veteran such as Dr. Cool. That's absurd.

I raise my hand and the chair recognizes me.

I say, "Shouldn't this say "tenured" faculty? Do we want assistant professors to vote on Senior Lecturers? Do we really think that all Assistant Professors are a higher rank than Senior Lecturers?"

The room, stuffed with sixty faculty members, is silent for a moment. Then, Dr. Linguist turns around to look at me, except she doesn't really look at me, just toward me. She says, "Yes, they are. I'm sorry, but that's just the way it is."

The chair nods. The motion passes.

I go to the departmental office. One of the administrators has been holding my son during the meeting with the sure hands of a grandmother. His small body is draped across her, his fist tucked into his mouth. I see my small boy lying on her chest, sleeping, and I shut the office door and cry.

January 2010

I come to the Bunker for the new semester, returning to teaching after a semester of leave. My textbook is in production. I did it all on my own, with no help from the Bunker. I'm proud of myself.

I walk into the Bunker's foyer, and the Board is down. Dr. Cool walks up to me and says, "Our names are going up. It's gonna happen today."

I say, "Is it silly that I'm so excited about this?"

In a world in which we always lose, we have finally won something. Standing next to Dr. Cool, I snap a picture of my name —well, Mr. Tall's name—on the new board, using my cell phone, and send it to Mr. Tall.

He writes back, "It's finally official."

I glance at Dr. Cool, her arms crossed, as she watches the letters adjust to accommodate us. And I wonder, *Is it, though? Can it ever be?*[1]

Introduction: A Manifesto for the Freelance Academic

In the new, corporate model of higher education, academics of all stripes, but most commonly those in contingent positions, find themselves pushed to the margins—of their departments, of their very institutions. If you're lucky enough to have a contingent, full-time position, you often still feel like an outsider. If you are an adjunct, then you almost certainly do. And even if you have a tenured or tenure-track position, you can probably see that the system you are part of is unsustainable. After all, higher education's future is rocky. You might worry that you'll need to relocate someday—and what will you do then, when there aren't any jobs to be found?

(That is, unless you are a lifeboater, willfully ignoring the chaos and pain around you. The term "lifeboater," used to describe the tenure-track academic happily riding the wave of exploitation, was coined by higher education blogger Jason Tebbe back in 2013: "These are junior scholars who don't bother thinking about the naked exploitation of a system where adjuncts are paid as little as $1,700 a course, and do just as good of a job (or better) as they do. In their minds, they won.")

Are your eyes wide open? Then welcome to the world of The Freelance Academic. I first wrote about this world in my series of columns for *Chronicle Vitae* of the same name, which ran from October of 2014 through September of 2017—three years tracking my transition out of the academy and into a career as a freelancer. That column, and the many essays that I've written since then, and a lot more writing besides, have now become this book.

This book tells the story of my transition from a patchwork, contingent career in academia to a new career: one where I decided to approach my academic career as a freelancer—with all the benefits that come with that approach. After all, the universities I worked for already treated me like a freelancer; it was high time I acted like one.

The decision to approach my academic career as a freelancer was incredibly freeing. And now that I've moved away from academia altogether, working completely for myself, I build on the freelance career moves I made when I was still in the academy. This book will teach you how to start making those moves, too.

———

But first: what drove me to look for something more than the work that I was doing day-to-day in academia? I came to a realization, one that many others have had as well. The realization went something like this.

As scholars and teachers, we work in overstressed conditions with inadequate resources, many of us hoping that somehow—someday—the academic world will right itself again. But the academic world isn't going to right itself again. It's changing, and it's not going to change back.

There aren't enough jobs for the large number of graduate students finishing up their degrees. The jobs are depleted for many reasons, but the main one is this: Even though college enrollment is higher than it used to be, colleges are relying more and more on contingent labor rather than full-time, tenured labor with benefits and job security.

To survive in this changing academic world in which

institutions treat (most) academics as disposable, I realized that we, as academics, have to change, too. Others, of course, had a similar realization, but since this is my book, I'm writing about mine. I do recommend you read other books, though, about how higher education has changed and how people have dealt with these changing conditions—these different perspectives will help you find your way. I've included a reading list at the end of this book.

One day, when I'd had enough, I wrote my opening salvo—a five-point Freelance Academic Manifesto, and I published it on my blog. Later, *Chronicle Vitae* (a branch of *The Chronicle of Higher Education*) republished it as a column. This was back in 2014.

The purpose of the manifesto was to help contingent professors (and all professors who are feeling woefully disempowered by their higher education employment) take some power back. Of course, the contingent professor I was mostly writing for was me. I needed help: a way to make work decisions in the new academic paradigm. I felt like I'd lost my navigational points, so I created new ones. As I wrote these navigational points, I relied heavily on a new community I built, using the alt-ac, post-ac, and adjunct communities I'd built on social media. I owe this community a large debt in compiling the manifesto, and continue to owe them.

The five points of this manifesto apply to you whether your contingent or tenured, whether you're new to the academy or on your way out.

1. Get paid for your work.

The first thing I told myself was this: Stop researching, writing, and editing for free. Get paid for your hard work. You deserve it.

After I'd edited yet another tenured colleague's scholarly article with no offer of reciprocation, I realized two things. First, I realized that I had a gift when it came to editing. Second, I realized that I could get paid for the work I was doing for free around my department.

Now, a lot of folks edit each other's work in academic departments as a part of their service work. Others do it to be collegial. Neither of those things applied to me. I didn't get service credit for the editing I did because scholarship wasn't part of my job description as a teaching-focused contingent faculty member. Scholarship was bonus work. And, after the third, fourth, or fifth time I edited someone's article without any reciprocation, I realized that my colleagues weren't being collegial. They were using me. One actually said, "I'm not telling anyone else how good you are at this, so I can keep you all to myself." How patronizing is that?

Seven years later, I get paid to help people place articles in top journals. Sure, I still help friends with their pieces, but only my real friends, and I know who they are. I don't let myself be used out of some misplaced hope that I'll be accepted into the cool club someday. The professors I help know they need editorial assistance. Their institutions give them professional development funds to hire editors—rather than an actual mentor, which would be better (but more expensive, I guess). So I fill that gap, along with other alternative academics like me. Later in this book, I'll talk more about what happened in that seven years between then and now.

I know getting started as a paid freelancer can be intimidating. Mulling over the plusses and minuses of working for yourself can help you make better decisions, as Kelly J. Baker noted in her 2014 *Chronicle Vitae* column on shifting her career to freelance writing ("To Write or Not to Write"), which I strongly recommend you read. In fact, I recommend that you read everything you can about how to start making money for the hard work you do. Gathering information about money, running a business, and what it actually takes to turn your skills into rent and food is the most important step you can take.

While you are taking good advice, please, do not listen to

people who tell you flat out that you can't do it. There are a lot of naysayers out there. I don't know what their problem is. Just ignore them. I know it's hard. Don't listen to them.

The heart of the getting-paid point is this: You are worth it. And, when you are an adjunct, earning a couple hundred bucks for writing a short piece in your area of expertise means groceries for your family for the month. Instead of taking on unpaid work in your department to catch someone's eye (maybe), earn some cash writing for a national audience and catch everyone's eye. Or spend some time working on a website for yourself to establish your national presence as an expert.

Speaking of that extra departmental labor: Getting paid also means when your institution asks you to take on extra work, you ask for extra money. When someone not in your institution asks you to do labor in your area of expertise, bill them, politely.

You have a living to make.

There is one exception to the get-paid rule: Love. If you truly love something, you can do it for free. But now and again you are required to reread smart things people have written that shine light on how the "love" of teaching and research has been used to keep academics poor. Rebecca Schuman, Jacqui Shine, and William Pannapacker have all written well on this subject.[1] They'll remind you how love can trick us into doing things for free when we should be getting paid.

Whatever you do, don't get snookered by the "love" thing. We academics have been told for so long that money sullies the life of the mind. I call malarkey. As Sarah Kendzior wrote in 2013 for *Chronicle Vitae*, "Should academics ever write for free? Maybe. Should academics write for free for a publisher that can afford to pay them? Never."

My theory about writing for free is this: There are a lot of great magazines out there that editors run for nothing. The staff don't make money, the writers don't make money—the entire enterprise is a labor of love. Sometimes, the magazine even loses money. What's the point? you might ask. The point is to publish stories that will make the world a better place. I write for magazines like that a lot. But if a magazine can afford to pay and it doesn't? That's exploitation, plain and simple. If it can afford to pay well, and pays poorly? Same. Mostly, you should never be shy about talking about money, and a publication shouldn't be shy about it either.

2. Live in a place you love with the people you love.

Here's when love should matter to your decision matrix.

Academia teaches you to move away from the people and places you love in order to be successful. Academia tells us that we have to be willing to move anywhere to find any job, otherwise we aren't dedicated enough.

When I was on the job market fresh out of graduate school, I turned down fancier jobs all over the country for my first contingent job. But I took that contingent job in order to be able to stay with my husband, to stay in a really nice place to live, and also to stay where both my and my husband's parents live. I traded the tenure track for my humanity. Unintentionally, way back then, I followed point number two on my manifesto. I'm so glad that I did. If I hadn't, I'd likely be where I am today—out of academia—but without the family I love around me.

The problem I faced out of graduate school wasn't one of choosing my family over my career. The problem is that academia, as a career, has become so broken that we have to make this choice in the first place. I'm an attorney: when I graduated from law school I had many, many choices of where to live and work.

That academia forces us to make the choice between our humanity and our careers is malarkey. Living away from the people we love is the opposite of living as a human being. If you have the choice, live with your family in a place where you enjoy living. Don't let anyone tell you that you are copping out by choosing your humanity over your academic credentials.

In a similar vein, if you want to have children, have children—

create new, small people to love. And if you don't, don't. And if you can't, you can have everyone read Elizabeth Keenan's 2014 column "The No-Baby Penalty" in *Chronicle Vitae* so you don't have to explain your private business.

3. When you find yourself being lured back to your department for a temporary gig, remember: They're never going to let you in the club.

Stop hoping that the department where you are contingent is suddenly going to recognize that you are awesome (despite the fact that you are, indeed, awesome). They're not going to suddenly offer you a tenure-track job. No matter how awesome you are, it just won't happen. I know that your friend's friend heard about a person at a college in Oregon where it happened (or was it Ohio?), but I'm telling you, it won't.

So long as you hold out a glimmer of hope that it will, your department will hold all the power.

And so long as they hold the power, you will keep taking on more free work, hoping that someone will tap you with a magic wand and make you a special fairy, too. It's never going to happen. Grieve. Accept. Move on.

Now, step back and embrace freelancing. Now you hold the power. You no longer have only one path to success—the path through traditional academic streams. Now you have a universe of paths.

4. Stop applying to academic jobs.

This one might seem a little crazy, so bear with me.

The job market is too expensive—temporally, emotionally, and financially. The chances of the perfect job being right around the corner are slim to none. The longer you're off the market working contingent gigs, the worse your application appears because departments prefer new Ph.D.s to ones with experience.

This is yet another way that academia is completely

backwards. I had a very hard time explaining this hiring paradox to my highly practical mother. "You mean your experience works against you? That's preposterous!"

Yes, it's preposterous. Fortunately, it doesn't matter. You're a freelancer now. So use the time and money you will save by not applying for jobs to start freelancing. Take a course on how to pitch ideas to writer's markets that pay, either through online courses or by hiring a successful freelancer friend to teach you. The course I took paid for itself within a week after I sold a story that I had workshopped during the course.

I know it's hard to let go of the dream of landing the perfect academic job. You might hear a story from a friend who knows someone whose cousin's mailman's niece finally landed a tenure-track position that was just right for her. You hear this story and think, Just one more round of applications, and that will be me!

It won't be you. I'm so sorry. You sound like someone who buys lottery tickets. Stop buying lottery tickets.

5. Remember that you are not alone.

Turning your academic knowledge and skills into cash is, itself, a skill. But there are people out there who can help you—hire an academic career coach, who specializes in helping people transition out of the academy. And, from what I've encountered on social media, we all believe in each other. The most amazing thing of all is how much they all want to help you. It's kind of miraculous. There will, of course, be jerks—the naysayers who will tell you that what you want to do is too hard or even impossible. Oh, jeez, please do ignore them.

———

Introduction: A Manifesto for the Freelance Academic

Is "freelance academic" the right term?

I received an email from a reader of my column once who told me, while she found my ideas about my career transition to be generally strong, she did not like the term "freelance academic" at all. Oddly enough, she had no problem with the "academic" part but rather with "freelance." I know that the reader meant well. Generally, her tone was supportive. But she spent an entire paragraph explaining how the word "freelance" "carries connotations of inferiority and lack of expertise or proficiency." It's a word people use, she wrote, "because they simply could not obtain a full-time paying gig."

Her recommended term? "Independent scholar." I've seen others use that phrase often enough, but it's not synonymous with "freelance academic." Independent scholar does not, at all, describe the work that I do. For example, I do not conduct scholarship anymore. I pretty much stopped writing scholarly work completely when I started writing for money. I have a few lingering scholarly articles coming out, but I'm not writing any new ones. (Unless you have a tenure-track position, the pay for publishing journal articles is terrible.) Thus, while "independent scholar" may describe very well what others do, it does not describe what freelance academics do.

But what about the second term in my chosen title, "academic"? In other debates over labels like "alternative academic" or "post-academic," I've heard other people express dislike of the use of "academic." Some of the arguments seem to suggest that when a person clings to the "academic" label, she is clinging to academia itself. Those arguments seemed persuasive to me, and they were made by people whose ideas I respect.

So I went to the dictionary. Oxford defines the adjective "academic," firstly, in this fashion: "of or relating to education and scholarship." I've already decided that scholarship, as such, is no longer for me.

But there's that other word—"education." I still do a lot with education. For example, I cover a higher-education beat in my freelance journalism (for money). I give talks that educate people about my areas of expertise, such as writing and disability studies. (I do that for money now, too, rather than just for a line on my C.V.) I write textbooks to help people learn. I work as a developmental editor to help writers finish their manuscripts and get them out to publishers—educating my clients about writing.

I'm immersed in education, and my academic training has allowed me to do this work. It seems to me, then, that "freelance academic" is just the right term.

———

This book is divided into three parts. Part I is titled "Coming to Be a Freelance Academic." Though full of advice, it is also a story: the story of how I left academia after eleven years and decided to make a career as a freelancer. You'll read about mistakes, failures, successes, epiphanies, things that worked, things that didn't, and everything you might want to know as you contemplate making a transition from higher education to a creative life outside of or adjacent to academia. As my friend Kelly J. Baker said to me recently, too many books and articles about alternative academic careers leave out the hard stuff. I'm leaving it in.

Part II, "Labor Conditions in Higher Education," addresses the foundation of alternative academia—the changing academic workplace. Job insecurity, low pay, long hours, heavy course loads: the life of a professor off of the tenure track is hardly what I was aiming for when I earned my doctorate. But life off of the tenure track inspired me to look for something else, and that something else led me to write this book.

Part III, "Practical Advice," collects the most solid advice I can give to current and former academics looking to live creative lives on their own terms. I know this advice won't work for everyone, but it worked for me, and for many of my friends, and I hope it will work for you.[2]

Coming to Be a Freelance
Academic

ONE

What Does It Mean to Be a Freelance Academic?

In May of 2014, I took a one-year, unpaid leave of absence from my contingent academic job. Over the winter prior, I'd earned something I'd thought I wanted very badly: promotion to a senior position with relative job security and fairly good pay, considering I would never have tenure. But the day that my department head called me to give me what was supposed to be good news, I thanked him quickly, hung up the phone, and cried. I realized that I'd been working eighty-hour weeks to achieve a goal I wanted nothing to do with. I hated my job. I hated my department. I hated everything about what I did.

I'd gone from loving my work to feeling trapped, overworked, and exploited.

How had that happened?

I did good work—good enough that when I requested a year's leave, they gave it to me. Unpaid, of course, and I'd have to cover all of my expenses, too, like health insurance, because I was contingent. While my tenure-track colleagues got their post-tenure sabbaticals fully-funded by the school, I paid for mine out of pocket. But I was grateful they gave me the leave. Because now I had a year to figure out if I wanted to go back at all.

I had a year to figure out if I could make it as a freelancer. This first section of *The Freelance Academic* shares my story of how I came to be a freelance academic.

―――――

HERE'S WHAT I DID RIGHT AWAY, EVEN BEFORE I FORMALLY LEFT FOR my leave. As soon as my request was granted—early in the spring semester—I started making some changes.

I changed my website's design from one that was basically an online C.V. for an academic to one that was an online portfolio about me.

I gave the website a title: *The Freelance Academic*. I'd been toying with that title for a while. I bought the URL (freelanceacademic.com), and directed it toward my website.

I started blogging a lot more. More importantly, I started blogging about more important things: I wrote about the state of higher education. About sexual assault law, politics, and my own experience. On the blog, I started establishing my areas of expertise.

These changes might not sound like much, but for a contingent faculty member, they were a big deal.

One important note: before I left higher education, I had some skills in web design. Once I decided to take my hiatus, I learned more. So when I say that I redesigned my website, I mean that I did it myself. And once I realized that I would be leaving academia for good, I decided to teach myself even more about website design, coding, and hosting. I studied tutorials online to add to what I already knew. Everything I studied was free. I strongly recommend learning how to design your own website so that you can maintain a professional web presence. If you can learn even more and offer website design as a freelance skill, even better.

What all of these changes amounted to was this: I dumped my online academic identity and claimed one as a freelancer—even while very much maintaining my contingent post at a university.

And, on the blog, I've stepped outside of the boundaries of acceptable academic discourse to engage in what one of my doctoral advisors once called "fist-waving" while he frowned at something I'd written. He wasn't using that phrase as a compliment, and ever since then, I'd felt hamstrung by the need to come across as measured and distant from the topics I examined in my academic writing.

But now it was time to create distance from academia so that I could be a better writer.

———

IT'S EASY TO LOOK BACK ON THIS TIME OF TRANSITION, NOW, YEARS later, and see my trajectory out of academia as smooth and simple. But it wasn't. The transition was filled with uncertainty, both career-wise and money-wise. One of the reasons I wanted to write this book is to document that uncertainty, to leave breadcrumbs for others to follow. I wanted to show exactly what I did (to the best of my memory), so that others can see that although it isn't easy, leaving higher education and starting your own career can be done.

One of the many problems with being inside of academia is that you cannot see the proverbial forest for the trees. As Rebecca Schuman has accurately put it (many times), academia suffers from a "cult mentality" that is hard to see until you step away from it. (Most) graduate students are taught by their professors to view the academy as the only viable profession for them. I was taught the same. In the newsletter from my own department, they print updates about the department's graduates—and they only send updates if you have landed a tenure-track job. If you have chosen a profession outside the academy, they don't want to hear about it. We are their failures, their ugly secrets—the graduate students who chose something else for our careers, or had something else chosen for us.

I don't, and didn't, feel like a failure. But in order to get there mentally, I needed to create some distance from academia. I first made some changes to my online identity—I professionalized myself as a non-academic, even though I didn't have a new profession yet. All I had was time off to figure it out. But one of my mother's favorite sayings is "fake it till you make it," so I started faking it, right away.

———

As I turned in my final set of grades and stepped away from my contingent teaching job, I discovered something important.

When you're a contingent academic, you are bifurcated into two professional beings. Half of you is the being the university insists you become. But then there is the remainder of you, what's left, the parts that the university doesn't want. Often, those parts are the very best of you. The researcher, if you are in a teaching position that doesn't value or support research. The innovator. The leader. All of those skills and gifts that the institution doesn't want—worse, wishes you didn't have?

What do you do with the leftovers? Squelch them down? Let them wither?

This bifurcation played out for me like this: There was the Katie who worked at my contingent teaching job, working fifty to sixty hours per week course planning, curriculum designing, lesson writing, student conferencing, and grading. I worked and worked and worked, hoping that I wouldn't actually feel bifurcated at all. I hoped I could fool myself.

It didn't work.

So then there was the Katie who worked on the side seeking to complete the teaching/research intellectual circle. There was no space in my contingent job description for the research and writing, unlike for my tenured/tenure-track counterparts. So I squeezed in writing on the side, in the evenings, on the weekends. I wrote novels (two), poetry, short stories (even published some), articles (I published so many! No one cared), conference presentations, and textbooks (three). My workweek added up to eighty to a hundred hours a week. It was, in a word, unsustainable.

I felt like I had a split personality. Like I worked three jobs. Like I was a terrible mother. Enter the surprise personal crisis and my request for leave.

And that was that.

To be a freelance academic is to recognize this bifurcation that we contingent professors face, and then to try to mend it. Yes, I worked for a university as a contingent professor. But I also wrote and researched. I realized that I didn't have to let any part of me be squelched or allowed to wither.

But I couldn't keep working hundred-hour weeks, either. That wasn't good for my health or the health of my family. But in order to stop, my goals had to shift. Indeed, the biggest change required to become a freelance academic is to recognize that, in the words of a dear friend from grad school, *They're never going to let you in the club.*

TWO

On Not Writing

In March of 2014, I asked for a one-year leave of absence from my contingent faculty job starting that May. That entire spring semester, I'd been struggling with my identity as a professor—I knew I needed to change things about my career, sure, but I also needed to change some things about myself.

I'd spent the entire school year working toward a promotion—from "assistant" contingent faculty to "associate" contingent faculty. I put together a full promotion book. I published research articles and gave talks at conferences, even though, as contingent faculty, my research didn't really count toward my promotion, not like it did for tenure-stream faculty. But I also knew that the people who voted on my promotion were all tenure-stream faculty, and they valued research as much or more than they valued teaching. I needed to make myself legible to them.

I taught my classes, crafting new curriculum along the way. I taught so well that my supervisor asked me to train the newly hired faculty (not that I got any extra money for that extra work). I was an expert. I was excellent. Surely, that would be enough.

I worked so hard, in fact, that I felt like I was finally earning my place on the faculty. I ignored, actively, the signals that told me otherwise. My pay was one-half to one-third what the tenure-stream faculty earned. I didn't have their other benefits, such as research assistants or research funding or even mentorship. And I didn't have job security. In short, I didn't have so many of the things that the tenure-stream took for granted.

I told myself, if I could just get promoted, I could ask for those things, and the department would give them to me. How could they not? I would have earned them.

When, in early December, the faculty voted to promote me, I felt like I had achieved something. Finally. But moments after, mere seconds, really, I realized that I'd been working toward an empty goal.

Promotion to what?

Who dreams of being promoted to yet another non-tenured job?

Congratulations, you've earned…another contract?

In the end, I didn't even get a pay raise. I got a new title, a renewed contract, and nothing else at all.

After working toward that one goal for so long, I needed to recalibrate. But I didn't know how.

Like most writers, I wanted to write about my experiences. But writing about my experiences as a contingent faculty member presented its own challenges, especially because I was still employed by a university. I didn't feel like I had the freedom to write about the politics of higher education while I was still mired in them because I was afraid I'd get fired for speaking out, for expressing any kind of opinion publicly. And at the time, I didn't know if I would still need my job.

How do you critique a system when you rely on that system to survive? All I wanted to write about was the higher education system that I'd been a part of for over a decade. My eyes were opening, and I wanted to share those discoveries. But I couldn't. I was stymied.

THE SPRING OF MY LAST SEMESTER TEACHING, MY COLLEAGUE AND friend Ariane and I were having a heart-to-heart over coffee in order to avoid grading papers.

She said, "I want to spend the summer writing a fun book, not academic research." A fun book to her meant a hardboiled mystery like something P.D. James would write. (James was her favorite author.) Ever since Ariane was a kid she only ever wanted to be a writer.

In response, I immediately said "me too"—but this wouldn't be surprising information about me, since I majored in English and have a master's in creative writing. Ariane, for her part, majored in biology. At the time of this conversation, of course, we were both law professors off the tenure-track.

We faced one of the challenges that non-tenure-track academics always face: If you have the luxury to have time to write, do you write scholarship with the hope of forwarding your academic career, or do you write something you might find more fun, and hope to publish it another way?

Of course, all of this writing presupposed that the stacks of papers get graded.

The bigger question is this: since non-tenure-track professors are no less driven or intelligent or educated than our tenure-track colleagues, what do we do with the remainder that is left over after we do the work required of us for our contingent jobs? What do we do with the remainder that our employers do not want from us, all that creative energy that they do not even want to know we have? Do we hope that our work will one day get us tenure-track recognition?

Or do we do something else?

At the time of this conversation, I'd been writing a lot, working hard to finish open projects (as a knitter, I would call these open projects "WIPs"—works-in-progress). Almost all of my WIPs were scholarly articles or conference presentations. Yet I was in a job that did not pay me for my research. Indeed, some colleagues (and I use that term loosely) grumbled that my research distracted me from my teaching, and they preferred that workers in teaching-track positions like mine didn't do research at all.

I realized, at that moment, that I didn't have a vision for the future of my writing at all. I had a mounting stack of unpublished book manuscripts (with no time to market them to publishers) and conference papers that would never be articles (because more and more I didn't see the point in rewriting them for journals). I wasn't even writing on my blog—it had been a year since my previous blog post.

So I found myself back to where both my colleague and I began our conversation: we were writers. In particular, writers who taught writing to law students and who didn't have a lot of spare time to write for ourselves.

Now that I had a premise to start from, I finished the stack of papers, and tried to create a vision for what would come next.

———

A FEW DAYS LATER, I GAVE MORE THOUGHT TO WHY I HADN'T BEEN writing on what is, essentially, my professional blog.

I came up with a very specific reason: fear.

Every time I sat down to give thoughtful written analysis of the topic that had been at the front of my mind, I self-censored out of fear. (For those of you who know me, you know me censoring myself at all is unusual.) I was afraid I would lose my job if I wrote about the inequities and other problems in higher education.

Fear was always with me when I would sit down to write about a topic that had been at the front of my mind, such as critical higher education studies or critical pedagogy. The future of higher education, and legal education in particular (since I taught in a law school). Although I'd already written on these topics for scholarly journals, I had not written on these topics in the far more personal forum of a blog. I was afraid to write about how working in higher education affected me, personally. How life off of the tenure track had changed my life, my career, my image of myself. I didn't know how to write these critiques from a position as myself, Katie, rather than from a position as a scholar, without putting my job on the line. So I didn't write at all.

I didn't know what to do to get around this fear that was hampering my ability to write, so I asked my friends for advice: "How do you blog about work inequities without losing your job?"

I got some great responses. The first response came from Lee Skallerup Bessette, author of the *College Ready Writing* blog published by *Inside Higher Ed*, which makes her first (tongue-in-cheek) response make sense: "Put your blog on the most visible platform you can—that way no one at your [institution] will notice." Shortly after, she followed up: "Seriously. Not one person at my [university] reads my blog."

Apparently, the first step to breaking through the fear-driven writer's block I was experiencing was to realize that I was the grain of sand in the ocean of words on the Internet. Easy enough.

Skallerup Bessette followed up with more substantive advice, advice that later responses to my question seemed to follow: "Be honest and always link it to the larger trends and structural issues."

By linking any critique I might make on my blog to larger trends, I would make my critique more substantive, less like a personal hatchet job and more like journalism (or even, gasp, scholarship). And it follows that this substantive critique would hopefully be protected by something like academic freedom (if academic freedom actually protected the jobs of contingent workers).

But really, a substantive critique must be less likely to raise hackles, right?

Skallerup Bessette's first bit of advice seems to be her most important: "Be honest." Critical higher education studies, it seems to me, must be grounded in honesty—in honest, clear-eyed assessments of the inequities that surround us every day in the academic workplace. These are the sorts of assessments that no one wants to talk about in faculty meetings or on committees (if one is allowed to go to faculty meetings or join committees). Thus, one person's "hatchet job" might be another person's "clear-eyed assessment"—especially when the person feeling the hatchet has tenure and the person giving the assessment is an adjunct.

When some of the most important evidence that critical higher education studies has to work with is the anecdotal experience of non-tenure-track faculty, all we have is our honesty.

And armed with this mindset, I started writing.

———

FINALLY, A FEW DAYS LATER, CLARITY STRUCK FROM THE OUTSIDE.

In February of 2014, *New York Times* columnist Nicholas Kristof bemoaned how academics don't participate as public intellectuals anymore ("Professors, We Need You!"). Of course, academics had plenty to say in response to his column (disproving his theory that academics are too quiet).

In case you missed Kristof's original piece—and you probably did because it wasn't terribly interesting—Kristof lamented the retreat by academics from public life. He wrote: "There are plenty of exceptions, of course...But, overall, there are, I think, fewer public intellectuals on American university campuses today than a generation ago." Kristof doesn't give a source for this change from then to now, just his gut. The reason for this change, though? Snobbery: "A basic challenge is that Ph.D. programs have fostered a culture that glorifies arcane unintelligibility while disdaining impact and audience. This culture of exclusivity is then transmitted to the next generation through the publish-or-perish tenure process. Rebels are too often crushed or driven away."

Anyways, Kristof was basically saying that academia, due to

its snobbish culture, is failing the world, and the world is worse off for it.

Suppose there are fewer public intellectuals on college campuses these days than there were a generation ago. Kristof doesn't suppose that something else might be the cause for the change, something beyond a culture of exclusivity. Something material, measurable. Something like the adjunctification of the professoriate that has taken place over the precise period of time that he points to.

Fortunately, Professor of Political Science Corey Robin handled this very issue in "The Responsibility of Adjunct Intellectuals" (*Al-Jazeera America*, March 2014). Robin, of all those who responded to Kristof's column, pointed out how the vast majority of professors do not participate in public life for one simple reason: they can't.

Indeed, Robin touched on the particular reasons why I, personally, had not participated in public life when I was a contingent professor, reasons that Kristof completely overlooks in his piece. Robin writes, "Writers and academics who fret over the fate of public intellectuals may think they are debating vital questions of the culture. But their discussions are myopically focused on the writing habits of a rapidly disappearing elite." The elite that Robin refers to? The tenured professor. If professors are participating in public life less and less, that's because there are fewer and fewer tenured professors.

Robin writes, "The vast majority of potential public intellectuals do not belong to the academic 1 percent [that is, tenured faculty]. They are not forsaking the snappy op-ed for the arcane article. They are not navigating the shoals of publish or perish. They're grading." Adjuncts don't have the time or the job security to participate in public life. They're teaching four or five sections across multiple campuses to keep food on the table.

Robin's piece addressed not only how overworked adjuncts are, but also the precariousness of their jobs. This lack of job security might lead an intellectual with otherwise interesting public ideas to keep such ideas to herself: "Nearly three-quarters of all instructional staff at colleges and universities today are not on the tenure track. They're insecure, contingent workers, an army of cheap and casual labor that make the universities go. While young writers can afford to do the kind of intellectual journalism we see at the little magazines, older adjuncts teaching five classes can't." They can't risk their jobs by taking a public stand that might cause their institutions to fire them. Institutions can fire contingent workers if they don't like what the workers say, and institutions, as we have seen, will do so. (I point out one such recent occurrence in Chapter 13, "The Racism False Equivalence Strikes Again.")

One of the most pressing issues in higher education today is the very statistic that Robin mentions above: three-quarters of higher education instruction is performed by contingent professors. And here's another problem: many of those best situated to write about this particular pressing issue are those who are most contingent. That is, those who are most afraid of losing their jobs in higher ed are the ones who are best suited to critique higher ed.

For many years, I was an "older adjunct," one with two children and a mortgage. I spent my first four years after graduate school terrified that I would lose my contingent job, playing a game of *Survivor* initiated by a department chair who told us that each year some of us wouldn't be rehired, that each spring she would review our teaching evaluations and only keep the best. It was a horrible way to live when I had a family depending on me.

One day, I realized that I couldn't do it anymore. One eye-opening moment occurred in the hospital. I had a premature baby, and a young resident doctor in the Neonatal Intensive Care Unit (an insensitive idiot) told me that my baby might have come prematurely because I managed my stress poorly while pregnant —as though I had some kind of choice given my work conditions.

Corey Robin's column asked an important question: Given our

precariousness and our heavy workloads, what can the world ask of adjunct intellectuals?

My answer is, so long as we rely on our departments for our entire livelihoods, not much. For me, something had to change. And that change became the Freelance Academic.

THREE

On Writing

MAY 2014

In May of 2014, I hit at a critical moment in my academic career. After eleven years teaching as an adjunct, all the while searching for a tenure-track job, I decided to quit searching. I gave up seeking something that I was never going to get and wasn't sure I wanted anyway.

Here's what I did instead: I wrote the "Freelance Academic Manifesto" (included in the Introduction to this book), and I decided I had better ways to spend my time and money than on the academic job search.

It wasn't easy, but I walked away—not only from the job search, but eventually from academia altogether.

When I gave up the job search, other things in my life changed as well. Essential to being on a perpetual academic job search is the requirement to publish as many articles as one can in academic journals and edited collections. The job search also requires presenting at as many prestigious professional conferences as possible. The last few years before I quit the job search, I ran myself into the ground trying to make my C.V. as impressive as possible, hoping to land a tenure-track job.

While publishing all of those words and traveling to give all of those presentations, I was also missing milestones: my older kid lost his first tooth while I was off giving a talk at a conference. I got to chat with him about it on FaceTime.

Guess what: It wasn't the same.

To use writer Rebecca Schuman's term, I was playing the "adjunct hero" (not a term of praise) hoping that my tenured colleagues would grant me membership in the tenure-track club. But finally, after eleven years, I figured out that that was never going to happen. How did I figure it out? I asked the person in charge—the chair of my department—and he said that I would never be considered for a tenure-track job. Ever. His words were like a punch in the face, but they were also incredibly freeing.

After that conversation, I requested one-year of unpaid leave in March of 2014, and left for it in May of 2014. Before I left, I had one more academic article that I committed to write, due in October of 2014. And then I was done. I stopped writing academic articles.

But I did not stop writing.

———

ONE AFTERNOON, I RECEIVED AN EMAIL FROM A REPORTER AT A popular magazine, asking to interview me about a current event: the forthcoming publication of Harper Lee's then-forthcoming book, *Go Set a Watchman,* and the apparent downfall of Atticus Finch as an American hero. I agreed to the interview. Before the reporter could begin the interview, I asked her a question: "How did you find me?"

I figured she saw something I wrote on social media on my blog.

No, she said. She found me through my research.

Many years prior, I published an article on *To Kill a Mockingbird* that took a controversial, critical stance on Atticus Finch. Based on that research article, the reporter believed I would be a good expert to interview about the new controversy surrounding the much-beloved character.

The next day, another reporter from another popular magazine called to interview me about the same topic. I gave another interview. Part of me found the entire situation hilarious, because my scholarship on the subject was published in such a minor venue and so very long ago. But the reporters were not wrong—I was indeed a good source. I did know what I was talking about (after I'd reread my own article).

How did they find me, though? And what, exactly, made me a good source? I did a few things right, things that anyone can and should do, especially any contingent faculty looking to transition to a life as a freelance academic.

First, I made my research publicly available by posting it on my own website and on open-access repositories that are indexed in Google Scholar. (My repository of choice is the Social Science Research Network, or SSRN.) By posting my research online and ensuring that it was Google-able, I'd made my research easy to find and had broken down the paywalls.

Second, I did something else equally important, and far more frightening. I agreed to the interviews in the first place. I agreed, even though I was nervous and afraid of sounding stupid. I was also afraid of being thought an imposter. After all, I was never a real professor, and I was not a professor at all anymore—right?

After a long conversation with myself after which I finally just told my inner critic to shut up, I answered the questions with all of the fake confidence I could muster. It wasn't long before the fake confidence turned into real confidence. And it wasn't long after that that I became the expert the reporters believed me to be.

I truly was the public intellectual speaking about one of the masterpieces of American literature.

Who, me? Yes, me. Frankly, it was weird. But at the same time, it was the most natural thing in the world. After all, why not me? I did the work. Why not me, indeed? Why not you?

I'm telling this story because I want to encourage you to put yourself in a position to engage publicly with your research. Freelance academics are perfectly aligned with the work of public engagement—but too often we worry that we aren't. We feel like imposter academics.

After all, if we were real academics, we'd have tenure, right? That is so not true.

———

ONE OF THE PROBLEMS THAT CONTINGENT ACADEMICS FACE IS THE double-bind of academic publishing: if we want to advance our academic careers, we must publish jargon-filled research in paywalled journals—work that we're usually not paid for because our jobs are teaching-track rather than research-track. Academics who bet on the insular system of higher education find themselves stranded when that system fails them, as it does most of us.

On the other hand, if we want to hedge our bets, to do work as freelance academics writing for the public in popular magazines, writing textbooks, or performing other non-insular tasks, then we run the risk of appearing non-academic, non-serious.

That's the double-bind: (1) Make yourself attractive to a field where you are unlikely to find work by publishing articles that are hard to locate, read, and understand. Or: (2) Make yourself attractive to fields outside of academia by publishing your work in an accessible fashion (easy to locate and easy to read)—but making yourself seem non-academic as a result.

Appeasing academics means alienating alternatives.

Journalist and former academic Sarah Kendzior points out how this double bind works in practice: "To 'count' is to preserve your professional viability by shoring up disciplinary norms. In most fields, it means to publish behind a paywall, removed from the public eye—and from broader influence and relevance. To 'count' is to conform."[1] Kendzior laments this standard of academic publishing: "But what 'counts' should be producing work of lasting intellectual value instead of market ephemerality. What 'counts' should be the quality of the research and writing, not the professional advantages you gain from producing it." Furthermore, accessibility on both the readability front and actually getting-your-hands-on-it front are equally important, as Kendzior pointed out. So much academic writing is hidden behind paywalls. And then, when a reader finally can download an article, the knowledge it contains is hidden behind field-specific jargon (some of which is completely unnecessary for the making of meaning).

This lack of accessibility means that often no one outside of a narrow field can put to use the important ideas that many, if not most, scholars are developing today. And yet, embracing this inaccessibility is required in order for your colleagues and potential employers to take you seriously as a scholar.

─────

THERE ARE A FEW STEPS THAT YOU CAN TAKE TO MAKE YOUR PATH TO public engagement easier while still maintaining your professional credentials. And if you have accepted that a unicorn of a tenure-track job is never going to come your way, all the better—because your path to public engagement just got a whole lot easier. You don't have to worry about what scholarly colleagues think. You only have to worry about what you think. That's what I did, and it was incredibly freeing.

After I gave up on finding a tenure-track job, I made sure that my scholarly writing was out there, just as it is, available on a public repository and on my website. And speaking of a website, I created an Internet presence for myself so people could have a sense of who I am as a thinker and writer—as a freelance academic. And then, I took that final step and starting writing my ideas for new audiences, for popular audiences. I did so by learning to pitch popular articles in my areas of expertise, and to write them, and, when appropriate, to get paid for them.

Step 1. Get Your Research Out There, Just as It Is.

If you have publications—articles, book chapters, books—they are likely not easily accessible on the Internet. You can change that. You can break down the paywalls. You can make it easy for readers to find your scholarship. Work with open-source repositories that are indexed on Google Scholar. It's actually easy once you learn how. The repository I use is SSRN—the Social Science Research Network. It's free to use with good instructions for how to upload your research, and you don't need to be affiliated with an institution to have an account. It is well-indexed on Google Scholar, which means that my work is easy to find by folks who might be searching for research like mine.

Once you create an account, you can start uploading PDFs of your articles, chapters, and even select chapters from your books. Warning: Some uptight academic publishers get really freaked out when you put a PDF of your own articles up on SSRN or other repositories because they hold the copyright to that particular printing of the article. They will send you angry emails demanding that you take them down. They'll email SSRN, too, and force that site to take them down.

This behavior is very annoying, especially since the work belongs to you, right? Don't worry. There's a very legal workaround. You have the right to make your work publicly available in two ways, even when your work is published by uptight companies:

First, you can upload the PDF of the actual journal article to your own website along with some language the publishers require you to use about it being an "author posting." So long as you are posting it to your own website, and not a repository, you can post the original PDF as much as you'd like. The problem, though, is that your own website is not well indexed in Google Scholar.

Second, you have a right to post on public repositories a PDF of your own creation. Such a PDF is called an "author's version" of an article—say, a PDF of the final Word doc that you submitted for publication. That work will be indexed in Google Scholar. Then, in the abstract in the repository, and on the PDF itself, you can note that the final PDF is available on your website. By the time you come across this book, SSRN might be long gone. But something else will have taken its place. Whichever repository you choose, know that you have the right to share your work with the world, and you don't have to rely on institutional access to do it.

Step 2. Create an Internet Presence.

If you want to be a freelance academic, then you need a website. You just do. Here are my suggestions, which you can take as you would like. Buy the URL (web address) that is your name. When I first started, I used WordPress as both my host and my content management system (CMS). That means that I used Wordpress to register my URL and to host my website. The URL I bought was my name, katieroseguestpryal.com, and that's the website I still use today. (Buying a URL, or web address, is not terribly expensive—like $15 a year.)

When you are building your website, start simply. Put your education and experience on one page—think of it as your online C.V. or résumé. But put your publications on a separate webpage so that they're easy to find. Then, on the page with your publications, link your publications to your SSRN page (or whatever repository you decide to use). You can also upload your author copies of your publications right there on your website, making it as easy as possible for readers to find your work.

After you start feeling confident about your website, try adding a blog. Blogs are a great way to test out ideas and share them. Blog posts can be short. You can turn off comments so you don't have to deal with trolls. (That's what I do. I allowed blog comments for about six months back in 2014, and then I turned them off forever.) You can automatically share your blog posts on social media—that's a function available through most blogging hosts. I highly recommend a blog. Indeed, after those Harper Lee interviews, I promptly wrote a blog post about them, adding more ideas that I couldn't share in the interviews, and adding my point of view as a writer, not just as an interview subject.

Speaking of social media: Twitter and Instagram have become great ways to network, share scholarship, and make connections. If you're intimidated by social media, find a friend who is not and sit next to her for an afternoon until you get the hang of it. Social media, such as Twitter, is worth using for the community you can build. And it is essential to creating your Internet presence.

Step 3. Share Your Ideas—Widely

Once you've put your research online and created an Internet presence, it's time to take the next step: rewrite your research into popular articles.

Whether your degree is in a STEM field or the humanities, you can find popular media outlets ready to pay you real money (though not necessarily a lot of it) to write about your area of expertise. You'll need to spend some time figuring out which sites are interested in which genres. And you'll have to learn how to pitch articles, and how to write the sort of pieces the venues want. You might not be able to make a living selling these pieces (after all, they pay bagels), but you can engage.

Remember, learning to be a freelance writer is hard. You have to learn a wide variety of new skills. I learned them by taking an online course. The course cost $200. I earned it back one week after finishing the course when I sold one of the stories I developed during the course. I'm still friends with the person who taught the course. Most importantly, I learned so much about the day-to-day lives of freelance writers: how much money we make, how to pay taxes, how to invoice, how to approach editors. When to write for free (never if they can afford to pay you, and sometimes if for a good cause and the

FOUR

Epiphany

THIS WEEK, I HAD AN EPIPHANY. GIVEN ALL OF MY WRITING, AND thinking, and writing about my thinking on being a freelance academic, I'm kind of embarrassed to talk about this epiphany—it seems so obvious now. Three months ago, in May, I look a leave of absence from higher education. Now, with some distance, I have room to think about academia, and how much I wasn't thriving there. I also, apparently, have room for epiphanies.

The epiphany came courtesy of my friend Sara, who gives me all of my epiphanies. The epiphany happened at lunch with Sara, when she spoke some "words" to me. Usually, my brain processes words. Words are a thing my brain can "do" and do well. But, as she was speaking, I couldn't understand what she was saying.

I kept saying, "What?" "What?" "Huh?" and she kept repeating herself in new and different ways, and her palm was twitching like she wanted to bop my head. Okay, maybe I'm imagining the palm part, Sara, but you have to admit you really were wanting to, or at least you were wondering if maybe the beer was affecting me more than it should have.

The point is, I was very resistant to the epiphany at first. I literally (in the literal meaning of the word) could not process the words Sara was saying to me because they seemed so strange and far-fetched.

But Sara stuck with me until the epiphany occurred, and all was well. No bopping.

But enough talking about this epiphany in the hypothetical. Let me tell you what I learned. Because it changed my life.

The Conversation

Just before the epiphany occurred, a law school sent me a recruitment email for a tenured position. The law school is located in a rather cool city, one located clear across the country from where I live with my husband and kids. At first I was excited to receive the email. But then I realized I couldn't take the job because it is located far away, and my family (my husband) can't move, and anyways I don't want to move. I really love where I live. And I really love the people I live with. Why should I move?

I told all of this to Sara, and she said, "Did you tell them you don't want to move?"

I said, "No."

She said, "Why not?"

I said, "Because."

She said, "Why not?"

I said, "Because."

She said, "Why not?" Then, *"Words words I couldn't understand words words I couldn't understand."*

I said, "???????????"

And then I had the epiphany.

The Epiphany

So, what Sara actually said to me was this: "I realize that you don't want to move, and therefore you don't want that particular job. So why don't you ask them to make the job into something that you do want?"

I couldn't understand how that would even be possible. I said some nonsense about distance-learning and the American Bar Association distance-learning standards and something else and something else and it all sounded a lot like blergity-blerg.

In retrospect, my problem was that I was suffering from a major failure of creativity.

For those of us living alternative-academic, post-academic, and freelance academic lives, we don't have set tracks that we must follow. Our tracks are, by necessity, only limited by our own creativity. They literally (there's that word again) are what we make them.

When we're confronted with a job offer or a gig that isn't quite right for us, instead of turning it down outright (like I did when I received that job offer), we have an opportunity to make the job right—through negotiation or other tactics. We have the opportunity to ask our counterparts to reconfigure what they're asking us to do so that we no longer have any of the worries or concerns that are holding us back from doing work we might be interested in.

But—and this is the hard part—we often have to make a request that is so far off the regular track that no one would ever think of it. I couldn't even figure out how to have a conversation with a friend about the kind of job that I could reimagine that job to be. In law, for example, distance-learning is so new and unusual that I couldn't even imagine a job in which I only commuted to the location every-other-week, say, and taught remotely the rest of the time. I couldn't even figure out how to suggest such a position to the institution that contacted me. My brain had been so well-trained that it couldn't drive off of the well-traveled path and forge a new one. The likelihood of the folks making the job offer being able to come up with creative solutions when I couldn't do so? Likely nil.

So: the burden of creativity on us is really high. But just because we have the duty of creativity doesn't mean we can't ask for the things that will make it possible for us to do the work we love to do.

We Can Bend Reality

I have a friend who is a professor of medicine, a faculty member at a major medical center, a mom, and an entrepreneur. She is, in her way, a freelance academic.

Recently, she said "no" to a last-minute, awesome interview with a major TV station in New York because she wanted to spend a rare afternoon with her kids. The interview would not have taken long, but arranging childcare and interrupting her day with her children would have been too difficult.

Probably. It seemed. To her.

Plus, the TV people needed her right then. (Welcome to television, apparently. Not that I would know anything about that.)

When she told me about her dilemma, later, and asked me for advice, I drew on my new epiphany. I told her this: "Next time, you can say yes. But you say it like this: 'Yes, awesome. Love to be on TV as an expert. You have an intern to watch my kids for 30 minutes, right?'"

She was like, "That's brilliant. The TV people would never have thought to provide childcare—even for twenty minutes—so I have to think of it for them." She didn't think they would have minded in the slightest. They would have been glad to have provided the childcare to have her on as a last-minute expert, in fact. But the problem was no one thought of the solution. The problem was a failure of creativity.

For my friend, that failure of creativity won't happen again.

Yes, the burden of creativity lies on those of us who take alternate tracks. But we have more power than we think we do to bend reality in our favor. We just have to start letting clients (including academic institutions) know what we need to get the job done.

If you need help coming up with creative solutions, you aren't alone. Reach out to your freelance academic colleagues and ask for help. If you have a coach who helps you, ask her. It's likely you aren't the first one to face the particular challenge that you are facing. Ask for some creative brainstorming help. I wish I'd spoken to Sara before I'd turned down that job offer. My doctor friend wishes she'd called me before she'd turned down that TV interview.

Next time we need to bend reality in our favor, let's help each other do it.

FIVE

Negative Capability

As I walked to my local coffeeshop this November morning to write, I saw a daytime moon. I quickly snapped a photo with my phone. The sun was, at the same time, very bright—in the photograph you can see the blueness of the sky, a spectacular, crisp blue that we only get in North Carolina after the summer's humidity has been chased away by cold.

I've lived in North Carolina off and on for most of my life, and I love it here. And I've lived in the Durham/Chapel Hill area off and on since 1994, and I really love it here in particular. I met my husband in Durham, and we're raising our kids in Chapel Hill. If I weren't so unsure about Western religion, I would completely buy into the "Southern Part of Heaven" thing they say around here when bragging about how beautiful things are.

When I saw this morning's daytime moon, with the sun and the moon both brightly visible in the sky at the same time, I thought about a person's ability to feel two ways about a thing at the same time.

This feeling-two-ways does happen, and it happens more often than we think. Keats called it "negative capability." On Twitter, Cornel West described it this way: "The ability to contemplate the world without the desire to try & reconcile contradictory aspects or fit it into closed & rational systems" (June 21, 2011).

You could just call this way of thinking "being open-minded," but maybe that's too simple.

Here's the point, today, though. I love Chapel Hill. I love The University of North Carolina at Chapel Hill. I'm a light-blue-blooded Tar Heel.

At the same time, though, I'm ashamed and horrified by the academic-athletic scandal going on right now—a scandal that is so complex and saddening and motivated by good and—at the same time—by the not-good—that it's hard to wrap your head around it unless you're in the middle of it.[1] I'm also bummed out by how the university is corporatizing its administration and killing its tenure lines and turning its faculty into adjuncts (including me). I'm bummed that UNC drove me from the career I chose by making my job one that I can't stand to do anymore, even though I'd worked to prepare myself to do that job for a decade. (I took leave from academia six months ago.)

I can feel both ways at the same time: love, and dismay. It's a thing that is possible.

My husband and I are both lifetime alumni association members of UNC. We are basketball season ticket holders. We take our kids to play on the quads and tell them stories about the old buildings—and the slaveowners whom they're named after. We're proud to have attended school here. I'd be proud to have my kids attend school here—and, at the same time, I would hope those buildings would all have different names by then.

As a nascent critic of higher education, I've been accused of hating higher education. Of even trashing it. But here's my question for you, my readers, and for those like me, all of us who write about higher education: Why on earth would I take time to critique higher education if I didn't care so much about making it better for everyone? For students—first and foremost—and for faculty, staff, and everyone who is a part of this extremely valuable public good?

I wouldn't. My mission is to make things better. If some dirty secrets get aired, you know what Supreme Court Justice Brandeis once said about sunlight being the best disinfectant. I'm doing the best I can with that mission in mind.

As a freelance academic, I do my work straddling two worlds: academia, and the world adjacent to academia. Sometimes that adjacent-to-academia world is at peace with higher education; sometimes it isn't. Sometimes my job is to help freelance academics see that they can work smoothly with institutions; sometimes my job is to show freelance academics how institutions do not have their best interests at heart. Usually, my job is to reveal that both can be true—at the same time.

SIX

Losing My Affiliation

My one year of unpaid leave was supposed to last until the end of the academic year, May of 2015—but I really like my direct supervisor at my institution, and I wanted him to have adequate time to hire my replacement. So as soon as I was sure I wouldn't be returning to my position as a contingent writing instructor, I let him know in mid-January.

I did not expect to have my university affiliation—and everything that affiliation entails—cut off within twenty-four hours of giving notice. I thought I would have more time—six more months, until the end of my leave, in fact—to transition away from my institution and, most important, to build a new professional identity.

Instead, I had to do it all in a day and a half.

I'm not complaining, not really. The life of the freelance academic is one I chose. But during that rubber-meets-road moment, I missed the "academic" part of that phrase a lot.

Ever since I started graduate school, I've been a freeway flyer, adjuncting at multiple campuses during the same semester (sometimes in different cities). But I always had at least one affiliation—at least one university credential. And being a part of an institution for over a decade gives you access to a lot of things that you don't know you will miss until they're suddenly gone.

Many of the challenges I've encountered during this sudden transition were surprising. Even more surprising were the solutions that I discovered. So in this chapter, I'll share my adventures in suddenly starting over, in the hope that they might help you in your journey from academically employed to self-employed, from academic to freelance academic.

The Easy Stuff

Technology: My institution provided me with a laptop, which was really great. But then I had to turn it in with very little notice —like, only hours. I had been planning for that eventuality, just not so soon. I know that other precarious academics living closer to the bone would have felt a sudden loss of technology more than I did. But ever since a public-records debacle rocked my institution, I'd been transitioning to my own gear for privacy reasons. I moved all my personal email to a personal email account, and I moved my personal files to a personal hard drive. I had my institutional hard drive regularly backed up to the Cloud (I use Dropbox), and so when it was time to hand over the laptop, I was ready. I found a solid, used MacBook on eBay, and I moved on.

Library access: Losing library privileges really set me back. I'm still working on figuring out the best way to replace that. When I lost library access, I had two journal articles in the editorial process for forthcoming publication. Losing my library access overnight meant that I could no longer check citations or update research. Here's what I did: I immediately reached out to a wonderful librarian (is there any other kind?) at my former institution's library and begged for her help. She reassured me that I could always come into the library and do research in person, using the databases there. I'm still reeling from her generosity. Of course, I will no longer have offsite access to those databases, so in that way I'm kind of sunk.

I have one plea to all of you in the freelance academic community: Share your own research on open-access databases or websites that you control. (See Chapter 3, "On Writing," for more details on how to do this.) I have shared all of my research on SSRN.com (the Social Science Research Network) and on my personal website. Posting all of your research on your personal website is great—but SSRN is indexed in Google Scholar. Posting your work on SSRN means that anyone like me, who does not have a library password, can access and cite your research.

The Hard Stuff

A university affiliation has been a part of my identity and my job title since I was in my mid-twenties. Losing it was the most amorphous of the challenges I've been facing, and, for a variety of reasons, the hardest one to deal with. That affiliation came up at least a dozen times in the first few days after I lost it. Immediately, I had to face the following tangible challenges:

Email signature: I had to figure out what to put there after I no longer had an affiliation. I had to accept that my work identity would be constantly evolving, and that's okay.

Online presence: I had to update social websites like Twitter, Facebook, LinkedIn, and Instagram. I also began to ask myself, Why, for the love of egg salad, are there so many of these to change? I also had to update my personal website and online C.V. to show my new status as a self-employed person. These website updates were something I hadn't been prepared to do yet. I didn't really have a title, or a business name, or even a job or business description. Clearly, this updating thing is also going to be an evolving process.

Business cards: I had to throw away a box full of university business cards, and then design and order new ones. What should be my logo? What should be my job title? As Admiral James Stockdale put it in 1992, "Who am I? Why am I here?"

Business structure: I had to incorporate my business and create a retirement account. I now have an S-Corp in the state where I live, and an individual 401(k) plan through that corporation. I rolled my former institution's retirement account into my new company's individual 401(k). (In Chapter 22, "Run Your Business Like a Business," I talk more about forming your own company and having your own retirement plan.) Listen, this took a lot of work, and it's still not done yet. Remember: I thought I would have more time.

And those were just the tangible challenges.

Then came the intangibles: I had books that I'd signed contracts to write, so I had to email my editors and tell them I was no longer employed by a university. I was afraid to write these emails: Would my editors be disappointed? Would they kill my contracts? (Answer: no.)

Obviously, I also needed to come up with a new job title that makes sense to other people. Then, I had talks that I was already scheduled to give at conferences—four, in fact. All of those conference name tags and programs were going to state my old institution. I was not looking forward to the awkward conversations that I would have with people after I struck out my institution's name—and do what? Leave the name tag blank? I needed to prepare an explanation, a description, *an identity*.

Because that's what happened. I suddenly lost an identity. That's the heart of the matter, isn't it?

And lastly, there were the intangibles that I wouldn't be able to predict. For example, how much would a loss of affiliation hurt my job prospects in the near future? If I had had time to ramp up my freelance work, to cultivate relationships and clients while still employed, would I have had an easier time transitioning from affiliated academic to unaffiliated freelance academic? At this point, I can only guess.

I can leave you with this: losing your affiliation will never be easy, no matter how much time you have to plan. I get emails from friends and strangers asking how hard it was to quit—and I tell them the same thing. At some point, you just have to do it. You can prepare, and you should, and then, one day, you must go.[1]

SEVEN

Reason to Believe

AUGUST 2016

WRITING IS BOTH EASY AND HARD.

For some people, one of my children, for instance, writing can be very, very hard. One of my children has an English language acquisition (ELA) learning disability that makes forming words and reading them difficult. For me, forming words has never been hard, even when I was very young. Being the mother of a child with an ELA disability, a disability so different from my own abilities and disabilities, has forced me to reckon with what I take for granted.

I take for granted that I will be able to put my thoughts into words, words that others will understand, indeed, that others will enjoy reading. One step further: I take for granted that others will enjoy reading my words so much they will pay actual money for me to write those words. Editors pay me, publishers pay me. I'm a professional writer.

For years, now, I've taken for granted that I would write things and other people would pay me for it.

And then, this week, two years after leaving my steady job in higher education to work full time as a writer, that changed.

Now Mary Lou loved Johnny with a love mean and true.
She said, "Baby I'll work for you every day, bring my
    money home to you."
One day he up and left her and ever since that
She waits down at the end of that dirt road for young
    Johnny to come back.
Struck me kinda funny, funny yeah to me
How at the end of every hard earned day people find some
    reason to believe.

From "Reason to Believe," by Bruce
Springsteen, Nebraska

At the moment, I'm at a turning point in my career, one that has me feeling uncertainty for the first time in a while—not the ordinary kind of uncertainty that I often feel as a person with anxiety disorder. Not the day-to-day kind. This is the big-picture kind of uncertainty. The step-back-and-reassess my life's purpose kind.

Two years ago, I took a year off from academia to sell a novel. I didn't tell anyone this goal at the time, except my husband. The goal seemed too far-fetched. But I succeeded—I sold the novel, and then the following year, I sold another one. And then, this week, my publisher cut me loose.

As anyone in publishing will tell you, publishers turn out writers all the time. That's just part of publishing. In fact, getting fired by my publisher could be considered a rite of passage for me as a novelist.

It didn't feel good, of course, and I was sad about it. I mourned the work I'd done for them, and the relationships I thought I'd built. And, of course, getting fired called everything I'd done into question. I blamed myself. I wondered what I'd done wrong.

And after I finished spinning myself in circles, I realized I was in much worse trouble than I'd originally thought.

Because then I stopped writing.

> *Congregation gathers down by the riverside*
> *Preacher stands with a Bible, groom stands waitin' for his*
> *bride*
> *Congregation gone, the sun sets behind a weepin'*
> *willow tree*
> *Groom stands alone and watches the river rush on, so*
> *effortlessly*
> *Wonderin' where can his baby be*
> *Still at the end of every hard earned day people find some*
> *reason to believe*

But I've been thinking about what it means to be where I am now, a novelist with no home for my books, and I think that maybe, it means nothing at all.

Maybe I should take fewer things for granted.

Maybe I should take a legal training course on current topics in disability law and take on a pro bono case.

Maybe I should finish that memoir manuscript that's been showing me how easy it really is to write novels.

Maybe having two children with greater-than-ordinary differences means that I need to cut myself some slack.

Maybe a trip up to the mountains is just what I need, even if it is for work.

Maybe writing is harder than I think it is, and that's okay.

Maybe I all I need is a reason to believe.

That's what we all need.

EIGHT

Bridging Academia

MARCH 2017

WHEN I LEFT ACADEMIA THREE YEARS AGO, I DEFINITELY HAD SOME guilt about letting my Ph.D. "go to waste." To make things worse, I'm a dual-degree holder—as a former law professor, I also have a J.D. And since I wasn't leaving academia to go into law practice (at least not full time), it was hard not to feel that, in quitting my teaching position, I was dumping nearly a decade of education down the plumbing.

Not a day goes by that I don't see my decision to leave higher education as the right one. No more trying to overlook the antics of a two-tiered system in which tenured and tenure-track folks (not me) are compensated well, while non-tenure-track folks (hey, that's me) are not, even though the latter do most of the teaching. No more worrying about whether one bad course evaluation would get me fired. No more worrying about job security, period. I have different worries now, but they aren't tied to the frustrating realities of contingent academic life.

But what about all of those years that I spent training for an academic career? I trained my mind to work in a certain way. I trained myself to have certain skills. I worked hard to develop a C.V.. And then I threw it away. Or did I?

I began writing my column *The Freelance Academic* back when I was contemplating leaving my contingent faculty job—for for my blog, and then for *Chronicle Vitae*. I wrote a five-point manifesto to guide my new career path. When things got confusing, the manifesto made things easier. In the manifesto, I gave myself five basic principles:

1. Get paid for your work.
2. Live in a place you love with the people you love.
3. Stop applying to academic jobs.
4. Remember that you are not alone.
5. When you find yourself being lured back to your department for a temporary gig, remember: They're never going to let you in the club.

————

IN RETROSPECT, WRITING THAT MANIFESTO WAS THE BEGINNING OF THE end of my traditional academic career. Sure, I told myself that if the "perfect" tenure-track job just happened to fall in my lap, I wouldn't turn it down. But we all know that perfect tenure-track jobs do not magically manifest in people's laps. They don't magically manifest at all. You can debate whether academia is a lottery, a merit system, a nepotism system, or a combination of all three, but what it isn't is generous. At least not these days.

So I wrote my manifesto, and I backed away, building a new career adjacent to academia with each backward step.

Then one day recently, I realized I wasn't backing away from something anymore. I was moving forward, with academia firmly in the rear-view mirror. After eleven years of teaching, I'd finally disentangled myself from that world.

Now I work for me. I own a company, one that's incorporated, and I make a living doing what I do.

But after three years out of higher education, I faced a bit of an identity crisis. Although I love writing the column *The Freelance Academic*, and the topic is meaningful to me, I wondered: Can I still call myself a "freelance *academic*"? Sure, I teach the occasional continuing-education course in creative writing at the local university, but I'm not in academia. Not anymore.

I wanted to know: What does it mean to be a freelance academic when you're no longer an academic?

Political scientist and higher education advocate Raul Pacheco-Vega recently referred to my role as "adjacent-to-academia," and I think that description fits best. I've realized that thinking of myself as "adjacent" has also helped me realize that my years in academia weren't wasted at all. In fact, it turns out that a post-academic career like mine can serve as a bridge between the academy and the nonacademic world—and in a great many ways. And serving as a bridge can have many positive effects.

The most obvious effect, for me, is the work I do regularly: writing for popular audiences to help create an understanding of ideas that are often locked away in the ivory tower. Researchers in higher education create a wealth of knowledge, yet so much of it never reaches audiences outside of academia's narrow silos. Lots of scholars have started sharing their own work and that of others for readers of popular media outlets. I urge everyone to give it a try. (Check out Chapter 3, "On Writing," in this book, which has information on how to get your writing out into the hands of the public.)

Jennifer Polk of Beyond the Professoriate, and others like her, serve as career coaches for former academics looking to transition out of academia. For those making such a career switch, having a coach—a bridge-tender, if you will—can be crucial to making that transition successfully.

There are many other ways to bridge academia — as a freelance editor, as an admissions coach, as a textbook author, and more. If you've left higher education with your training in your back pocket, you haven't thrown anything away. You've prepared yourself well for a life of your own design. The rest of this book will give you ideas for how to build that life.[1]

Labor Conditions in Higher Education

NINE

Quit Lit Is About Labor Conditions

THE DISMAL STATE OF THE ACADEMIC LABOR MARKET HAS BEEN critiqued for years at this point. Those of us who began our doctorates before contingent labor had become the norm, back when there were still jobs to be had, finished our doctorates with no hope for a career in sight, not really. So we worked in contingent positions as visiting professors (if we were lucky), lecturers, or adjuncts. We usually made very little money. We had no job security. Some of us, or most of us, left. Some of us who left then wrote about it.

These essays about leaving academia became a genre, and the genre gained a name: "Quit Lit," which was, as far as I can tell, first applied to leaving-academia essays by higher education critic Rebecca Schuman in *Slate* in October of 2013.

The Quit Lit Foremothers

Rebecca Schuman wrote an early piece of academic quit lit, also for *Slate*, in April of 2013. In the piece, titled "Thesis Hatement," Schuman does three main things: she warns readers not to go to graduate school. ("Don't do it. Just don't.") She tells them why. ("I now realize graduate school was a terrible idea because the full-time, tenure-track literature professorship is extinct.") She also describes the pain she suffered as she trained for a career that was never going to manifest. ("During graduate school, you will be broken down and reconfigured in the image of the academy. By the time you finish—if you even do—your academic self will be the culmination of your entire self, and thus you will believe, incomprehensibly, that not having a tenure-track job makes you worthless.") These three arguments—warning, critique, and description of one's suffering—comprise the heart of all quit lit. Not every essay has all three arguments, and most essays focus on one.

One of the most attractive qualities about Schuman's essay is that she doesn't hedge. She doesn't say that there are "fewer" jobs. She says that there are no jobs. Because, as she points out, in her discipline there were one hundred and fifty applicants a year for six positions world-wide. With those numbers, the difference between few and none is no difference at all.

Despite its grimness, Schuman's essay is inspiring as well. She inspired me to write and publish my first non-academic essay as I was inching toward the exit of higher ed. The essay I wrote was a litany of the tiny, daily humiliations of being a contingent faculty member (and it serves as the prologue to this book). But, in retrospect, that piece was also setting up the evidence that I would use when I finally quit. I was able to point to that essay to prove why life as contingent academic labor in the contemporary university is, for the most part, as untenable as Schuman described. It was worth quitting.

I quit, and I wrote about it. I also connected with other writers who wrote about quitting around the same time I did—with Schuman, Kelly J. Baker, Sarah Kendzior, Elizabeth Keenan, and others I'm sure I'm forgetting here over the years. We wrote about the terrible experiences of being precarious in academia. We were mocked for doing so, sometimes, by people both inside and outside academia. We were told to "stop complaining"—either our poor job situation was our own fault (people inside the academy usually said this) or we didn't have so bad (people outside the academy usually said this). We had a variety of goals, sometimes simultaneously: to help others make better decisions than we did (don't go!) and to improve academia with thoughtful critique. We were mostly women—because, as Kelly J. Baker points out in her 2018 book *Sexism Ed*, the academic precariat is predominantly women. We are mommy-tracked. We are trailing spouses. Although we are hard workers, we are not "brilliant" like men are, as Baker puts it, so therefore we don't deserve tenure-track jobs.

Over the years, my quit lit friends have gone separate ways and found success in their new chosen fields: journalism, writing, real estate (and writing!), and more. The fire that drove us away from the academy in the days of the rise of the academic precariat —and the attendant rise of quit lit—had cooled to a slow burn. Because that's what drove quit lit in the beginning. Quit lit, at its heart, was a labor critique.

Insider Quit Lit

Five years pass. In February of 2018, the *Chronicle of Higher Education* published a new quit lit essay, one that garnered a lot of attention. Erin Bartram, a history Ph.D., originally published the essay about leaving academia after years in a contingent faculty position and on the job market (originally published on her blog: erinbartram.com). Titled "Why Everybody Loses When Someone Leaves Academe," the essay opens with her final failure on the academic job market. She leaves her office in her department (she's a history professor), described with all of the nostalgia a professor can muster, including a reading lamp and fountain pen ink.

And then her essay takes a surprising turn. Her indictment is not one of the dismal labor market, but rather one of her field (or any field) that allows such losses to continue unabated—the loss of scholarly colleagues—whose contributions to research will be lost forever. She writes, "Even in our supportive responses to those leaving, we don't want to face what's being lost, so we try to find ways to tell people it hasn't all been in vain." Later she writes, "We don't want these people to go, and we don't want to lose all the ideas floating around in their heads, so we say, "'Please give us those ideas, at least. Please stay with us just a little bit.'" And she's right; when I left academia, my former colleagues said similar things to me.

Like Schuman, she talks about the pain of losing the part of her identity that she trained years to build: "I've lost a huge part of my identity, and all of my book-learning on identity construction can't help me now." And perhaps most poignantly: "I don't know what I'm going to do. I don't know what I'm good for."

The piece garnered a massive response. There were response essays in the *Chronicle of Higher Education* itself, which noted that Bartram's piece went viral; that it "generated a vesuvian outpouring of responses"; that the original blog post was read at least eighty thousand times.[1] By any metric, Bartram's piece struck a chord with readers.

Obviously her essay appeals to outsiders who have quit academia. But Bartram's piece is radically unlike Schuman's and others in a particular way that makes it appealing to more than just those who have been forced out of the academy.

Bartam's essay provides no critique of the academic labor market, not really. It does not describe poor working conditions—on the contrary, her conditions seem to have been good. She had an office, and a desk, and a lamp. She had colleagues that she will miss. Perhaps her conditions were poor, but those poor conditions are not described in this essay.

And for that reason, her essay appeals to insiders, those on the tenure-track and others who approve of the academic status quo (the status quo that harmed Bartram herself), because it maintains nostalgia for the academy itself. This nostalgia does not appear in Schuman's essay and most other quit lit. Bartram doesn't speak to labor conditions and how working as contingent faculty can be back-breaking and poverty-inducing. She speaks only to how much she'll miss her research and her chosen field, not to how much she was pushed out by those who stay behind—by that field itself.

Indeed, weirdly, she still speaks of her chosen field as though she were a part of it. She uses the first-person plural "we": "We don't want these people to go, and we don't want to lose all the ideas floating around in their heads." In this essay, Bartram (whether intentionally or no), still frames herself as an insider. No wonder the essay was so appealing to so many. Although buried in her essay was a strong message of suffering, she did not bring a strong critique of higher education: "What would happen if we, as a community, stopped saying 'he's gone to a better place,' bringing a casserole, and moving on. What would happen if we acknowledged the losses our discipline suffers every year? What would happen if we actually grieved for those losses?" That's not a critique. Those are words of comfort for those who've harmed you. As I read the piece, I wondered, *Does she even know why she lost her job? Does she want to hold those people and systems accountable?*

A Practical Labor Critique

If quit lit is about labor, then the best quit lit published in the last year wasn't about quitting at all.

In April of 2018, *Chronicle Vitae* republished a blog post written by Annemarie Pérez (blog: *citedatthecrossroads.net*) on how an adjunct's current department can do practical, material things to help that adjunct further her academic career—rather than continuing to exploit her. Pérez's piece, "Instead of Gaslighting Adjuncts, We Could Help Them," was one of the few recent pieces I've read in *Chronicle Vitae* on adjuncting issues that still burned with fire about the dismal academic job market and the attendant labor exploitation.

Quit lit does not tend to have the happy ending that Pérez's essay has—she landed a tenure-track job after many years of adjuncting and with the mentorship she found in her temporary department. Other pieces over the years have had a very different outcome: faculty, usually contingent faculty, have left the academy, disillusioned by the mistreatment and exploitation they experienced in the departments that exploited them.

But don't be fooled: Pérez's essay is an indictment all the same. The essay provides a practical guide for tenured faculty who work alongside adjuncts. Pérez pulls no punches: "We don't have to just wring our hands about how terrible the situation is, or, worse still, say the job market has always been terrible and those who are adjuncts should never have started a Ph.D. if they weren't willing to be exploited." Here, she says, do this instead. Mentor, guide, help. The jobs are there, actually, if you are willing to help instead of pretending not to see.

Those people in Bartram's essay who bring casseroles? Those are the people Pérez is taking aim at.

Bartram's piece had heart. But in the end, it coddled the powerful. Pérez's piece called them on their gaslighting and provided concrete steps for fixing the problem my friends and I have been writing about for five years. But eighty thousand people haven't read Pérez's piece because it isn't an encomium of the academy.

The academy doesn't need encomiums or casseroles. It needs practical labor critiques like Pérez's. And it still needs quit lit—stories from marginalized higher education workers who, because of career change or some other reason, finally have the ability to tell them. If you are getting started as a freelance academic, perhaps the first thing you should write is your good-bye letter. Even if you never share it with anyone but yourself.[2]

TEN

The University Is Just Another Client

WHEN YOU'RE A CONTINGENT FACULTY MEMBER, IT IS IN AN institution's best interest to get you to do the most for the institution for the least amount of money. You have a transactional relationship. It can be hard, when you're the faculty member, to think of your job that way, when we've all been trained, through years of graduate training, to think of higher education as a calling, rather than as a job. But when you're contingent, that's exactly what you have—a job.

In fact, when you're contingent, you often don't even have a job. You have a gig.

Contingency has turned higher education into just another part of the gig economy. It's a sad state of affairs, but it's here to stay. My job is to help you navigate these less-than-ideal labor conditions in a way that protects you and your livelihood.

———

MANY TIMES OVER THE PAST FEW MONTHS, I'VE HAD SOME FORM OF A conversation I'm about to describe with non-tenure-track colleagues—and even some tenure-track ones.

When I say "non-tenure-track," I'm referring to all contingent employees of an institution, including adjuncts, staff members in faculty-like roles (i.e., alt-ac and staffulty roles), and contingent instructors in full-time positions. Often, these different groups have different concerns. But for the purposes of this chapter, I hope that all of them can find something useful from the ideas I'm about to share.

I know I'm going to sound like I'm preaching with the fervor of the converted. But I'm not converted: I'm simply more aware now of university power dynamics (bless my former naïve heart) and how to use them, and I want my friends to share that awareness.

Here's a typical situation.

I was having coffee with a friend Elle early on a Tuesday morning. She'd been searching high and low for ways to break through the contingent ceiling at our institution. She was teaching on a nonrenewable contract in the same department as I was, and she wanted to find a way to encourage "them" to hire her on a more permanent basis when her contract expires.

With that goal in mind, she'd taken on more service work, she'd started teaching an extra course (for no extra pay), and she was letting more students into the classes she already teaches—hoping that someone in a position of authority will recognize the awesome work she was doing.

I was stunned by how much extra work she was describing. Since I tend toward bossiness, I consciously forced myself to just ask questions (and no, not leading questions), to get a full sense of what she was doing.

Finally, I asked, "Why are you doing all of this extra work?"

And finally, she said something like, "I really want them to keep me on after my contract ends."

There was so much hope, and pain, in her voice, that I wanted to give her a hug. But I refrained. She didn't need a hug. She needed someone to tell her that our department was never going to renew her contract.

She wouldn't have believed me. Who was I? Just another

contingent faculty member. But when I'd been in similar shoes to hers, overworking myself, hoping these same people would let me jump over to the tenure track, I did a very scary thing and asked our department head if I would ever be permitted to do so.

He told me I would not.

Bursting that bubble hurt, but it also cleared my vision.

Elle needed to ask that hard question. I couldn't answer it for her. If you aren't sure if overworking yourself will pay off, you need to find out. And don't worry—asking won't hurt your chances. Your department might prefer to keep you in the dark in order to get your free labor, but getting the truth can only help your career.

———

MY FRIEND ELLE WAS DOING THE CONTINGENT FACULTY EQUIVALENT of writing a piece on spec. "On spec" is a term that journalists use to refer to when editors ask newbie journalists to write pieces prior to being hired—because that's usually not how it goes. Usually, you pitch a piece, the editor accepts it, and then you write it. Usually you don't do the work not knowing whether you'll be paid, not knowing whether it'll help your career.

Except what my friend described isn't like an article you write in your free time. She was talking about her whole career.

As a contingent faculty member, you work your whole career on spec. Every class you teach, every grant you write, every article you publish—they're all on spec, because you have no job security to back you up if a project doesn't pan out. You work and work, hoping some person in authority will give you: (a) more money, (b) more job security, (c) more job respect, or some combination of (a), (b), and (c).

But then it never pans out. As those of us who've been at this for a while know, giving administrators your work for free does not inspire them to reward you. More often the extra work backfires and inspires administrators to turn your previously volunteered work into new job requirements. Suddenly what you did as a favor becomes a rigid job expectation.

Fortunately, I have a solution. It begins with a shift of mindset —from that of employee to that of freelancer. As a freelancer, your institution is just one of your many clients. That means you need to spend your extra time and energy on projects that earn you both money and respect outside of one particular institution.

———

You know who works on spec a lot? Freelancers. But they (usually) know how to do it while preserving their time, finances, and mental health.

Non-tenure-track faculty are the freelancers of academia, and we need to start acting like it. Look at it this way: Your university has basically already said that you are a freelancer. You are already working job to job—gig to gig. That's what a year-to-year contract means. Or in the case of my friend, a terminal contract: She took a job with a client, and when that job ended, so did the client relationship.

Fine.

But if that is the case, then your institution will just be one of your many clients. Freelancers don't make a living hoping one client will keep hiring them over and over. They form relationships; they find other clients. Non-tenure-track faculty need to do the same. And if you are a tenure-track professor reading this, and you have noticed that higher education might not be able to sustain you either, then I'm also talking to you. I firmly believe that it's time for all of us in higher education to diversify.

So instead of giving away your work for free, hoping for a reward that will likely never come—embrace the freelancer ethos. Take some time to work for yourself.

Often when I suggest that we should apply this client-based strategy to academia, however, I get pushback. For some people, this strategy seems disloyal to their institution—like you're cheating on your significant other. But you can only be loyal to a company that is loyal to you. And if you are non-tenure-track faculty, your institution is rarely going to be loyal to you.

In order to make time for yourself, you'll need to dial back the "adjunct heroics," as writer Rebecca Schuman has put it. That is exactly the advice that I would give my friend: Decline unpaid service work that won't be rewarded anyway. Keep office hours to the bare-bones requirement. Set limits on your letters of recommendations for students. And deflect all the guilt that others will probably lay on you—guilt from faculty, from students, and even from yourself.

——————

IT TOOK ME A WHILE TO ADJUST TO THE FREELANCE ACADEMIC mindset. I really, really wanted to feel loyalty to the institution where I worked, and then to the next institution where I worked. I wanted to find a home. But each time, the same thing happened: I was told, directly and indirectly, in large and small ways, that I did not belong because I was non-tenure-track. I felt betrayed and hurt. I cried, a lot. (You are probably very stoic and do not cry. I'm happy for you.) When these slights and put-downs and exploitations started happening at my second institution, I didn't feel like I'd been hoodwinked. I felt like I'd made the same dumb mistake twice, and I blamed myself.

The second time, I changed my mindset completely. I couldn't quit outright—my family needed my salary. But I was ready to start planning an exit strategy. And I was ready to start making my life better right away, before I quit. Enter the freelance mindset. My institution, I decided, was just another client.

Say you've adjusted your mindset. You're ready. Your institution is Client A. But it's time to look around for other clients, too. Who else is there? That might seem like the hard part, so bear with me for a minute.

Think about which of your skills are marketable. Sit down and write a list of every possible skill that you have. This is not the time to be humble. You might not know who to market your skills to, or how, but that's OK. You can start learning those things. You're an academic. You know how to research.

You need to transform your C.V. into a résumé—or various résumés for different types of work you might be interested in doing. When I did this myself, it was—and I'm not kidding—so much fun. I used Rachel Leventhal-Weiner's 2014 article on résumé writing for academics for guidance ("Don't Fear the Résumé," published in *Chronicle Vitae*). If you try to make your skills list and your résumé and have trouble—a totally understandable problem—hire a post-academic coach to help you. Together, you can figure out what you're good at that can earn you money.

Most important, at least for your mental health, recognize that you are not alone. Build a community, whether online or off, of others who are trying to do work similar to yours. That community will help you network into new opportunities and will reassure you when you start to doubt yourself. There are freelance networking communities that you can join. I subscribe to a newsletter called, unsurprisingly, *The Freelancer*, which helped me learn about setting rates, dealing with clients, and more. And you can join the Freelancers Union to learn even more about the practical side of freelance life. They even have health and other kinds of insurance for their members.

Remember that moving into the mindset of a freelance academic does not mean that you give up your job teaching on a campus. It just means that you approach your relationship with your institution differently. You no longer belong to them: They belong to you. Once that shift happens—and you'll know when it does—there's nothing more empowering.[1]

ELEVEN

The Ugly Side of Academia

I CAME ACROSS SOME WORDS BY JAMES BALDWIN RECENTLY: "THE price one pays for pursuing any profession, or calling, is an intimate knowledge of its ugly side." Now, Baldwin was talking about race, and masculinity, and his relationship with Norman Mailer. The entire essay (published in the May 1961 issue of *Esquire* magazine) is breathtaking, and you should read it. Baldwin touches on how those who are marginalized and oppressed know a lot more about those in power than those in power know about those who are marginalized and oppressed. And Baldwin does it the way Baldwin does—with precise, cutting, yet lyrical language that flips your world upside-down.

I was in academia for eleven years. If you count my master's program, when I had to fend off harassment by two different male professors, and law school, when my favorite professor was denied tenure for being a woman and another professor (who was in his sixties, and whom I didn't like) married one of my classmates (who was in her twenties, and whom I didn't know well), even longer.

The point is, I've pursued this profession of higher education for most of my professional life. And, because of my experiences —as a woman, as a disabled woman, as a disabled woman in a slew of contingent positions—I can see that this profession is really ugly. But I'm wondering, today, is academia any uglier than any other profession? Or do I just see its ugly side because I am so intimate with academia? And further, does everyone in academia see academia's ugly side?

Is it possible for a white, male professor on the tenure-track at a top university to jamble along and never ever see the ugliness of academia the way that marginalized faculty do? For it to actually not be ugly for them at all?

The other day, a super-tenured (that's a technical term) male professor in my division actually asked one of my non-tenure-track colleagues just how much we made as a salary—because he had no idea. Now, I know how much this tenured male professor makes, because it is public record. Also, I took that public data and created a spreadsheet to compare salaries by race and sex. The results, as you might imagine, were not at all surprising. Women, and people of color, make less money. We are also overrepresented in the contingent ranks.

I would never, however, have had the gall to ask a tenured professor what his salary was. I also would have been afraid of being fired.

When this white, male, tenured professor learned what we earn each year, he dropped an f-bomb out of shock, apparently. The professor just had never considered that we would be paid so little for all the work that we do. It was his privilege to never think about it. Whereas, for the rest of us, we have to think about money all the time.

So I think that yes, non-tenure-track faculty, and certain others on the tenure-track, like white women who get denied tenure for not being masculine enough, and women of color who get pushed out for not being "respectful" enough (yes, these things happen all the time in top-secret, non-appealable tenure votes), we really do get to see an uglier side of academia.

Because we have to think about it. We're forced to stare the ugly side in the face every day, even as we do our work, teaching, writing, and trying to make the world a better place.

Despite this work, recently, a friend I respect told me that she was concerned that my writing on academia came across as though I had "sour grapes." She was talking about all of my writing on academia: on my blog, on social media, and in my columns in magazines.

She did have some reason to be concerned. She felt like she had to bring it up because we are entering into a business endeavor together. And keep in mind, she was sincerely, truly worried about hurting my feelings. Also, you can see her perspective: Is a crank a good spokesperson for your business?)

But I was truly surprised that she viewed my words as sour grapes—or as anything that could reasonably be perceived as such—in the first place. I actually think I'm kind of Pollyannaish, once you get past the "we need to stop deluding ourselves" bit. I don't wallow in misery, and I'm very practical. The point of the freelance academic endeavor is not just to identify problems with higher education, but to find ways to fix them as well.

After our conversation, I looked up "sour grapes" in the OED. I learned that the phrase derives from one of Aesop's fables, "The Fox and the Grapes." These days, it refers to a situation "in which someone adopts a negative attitude to something because they cannot have it themselves." So I guess my friend is saying (and I'm inferring here) that since I didn't get a tenure-track job, I have sour grapes towards higher education.

But she's wrong. And worse, she's not alone. A friend of mine just told me a story where a former colleague, someone still in higher education, but miserable, asked my friend if she were "jealous" of the former colleague's tenured status. When my friend told me this story, we couldn't believe how, after all the public writing we've done on leaving the academy, someone could still think we wished our careers had gone differently, in particular, that we had gotten tenure.

Rather, I feel like I narrowly escaped by not landing a tenure-track job. There's something rotten in the state of higher education, and if I'd moved my family into that dying kingdom, where would I be? Hoarding my meager riches and stomping on contingent faculty? Or worse, pitying contingent faculty and wringing my hands because there is nothing I can do—after all, the problems are structural and too big to fix? I'd probably hate myself—if I were self-aware enough to know what I was doing.

Coincidentally, I've been working on figuring out how to briefly answer this question: "What do you do, now?"

Answering this question isn't about figuring out how other people see you. It's about figuring out how you see you—and what you want to be for yourself.

I know one thing for certain: I do not want to be a tenure-track professor.

The academy cannot give me anything that I cannot discover on my own. That's not sour grapes. That's waking up. That's what it means to be a freelance academic.

Now: Soon I will address, in a more hopeful fashion, the wonderful open pathways that higher education holds for us. Because that hope is there. Those pathways are there. Thinking creatively about learning, teaching, finding making sharing knowledge—we have to do those things. And we can.

Also, we have to eat. I'll talk about that, too.

TWELVE

The Invisible Adjunct Hero at Kentucky

I READ A STORY IN THE *NEW YORK TIMES* ABOUT STOLEN EXAMS AT the University of Kentucky, in which an undergraduate student crawled through an air duct to steal a statistics final in order to cheat. ("Student Arrested After Crawling Into a Duct to Steal an Exam," May 4, 2017.) The student let another student into the building, and then they were busted by the professor when the professor returned to his office after a "late-night meal" and found the students there. The students, surprised by the arrival of their professor, took off running. But when one of them realized that the professor would be able to recognize him in class, he returned and confessed.

All of this took place around two o'clock in the morning on a Wednesday.

A few things about the story struck me as odd. First, in the article, the professor was never referred to as "professor," but rather as "instructor"—and the Times was very, very careful to never use the word "professor": "The instructor at the University of Kentucky, who was working very late, had gone out for a midnight meal and returned just in time to derail the plan, according to a university spokesman."

Second, the late hours of the events struck me as odd as well.

Why was the professor at work so late—obviously his students didn't expect him to be there. Sometimes professors teach late—when they teach, say, graduate seminars that run into the evenings. But the large, introductory courses for which a student might bother to steal an exam? Those don't usually take place late. And stealing an exam? That's not the sort of thing you do for an upper-level seminar.

Someone not attuned to higher education would miss these details. Someone who hadn't spent a career as a contingent faculty member wouldn't make the same deductions I did, deductions it only took a quick internet search to confirm. Of course the "instructor" was a contingent faculty member. Of course he was.

After I conducted a little research, I figured out which course that the students were stealing the exam for: "Statistical Methods and Motivations: Introduction to principles of statistics with emphasis of conceptual understanding." And the professor listed for this course? His name is "TBD." (Actually, the professor who busted the students is named is John P. Cain—but his name is not on the course listing.)

This news story highlights the lives of contingent faculty, if you know what you're looking for. It shows what we do. We work too much, at wacky hours, often in shared offices, teaching introductory classes over and over again, with courses, schedules, and locations that are perpetually "TBD."

Contingent faculty are the TBD. As Crash Davis put it, in the movie *Bull Durham*, we're The Player to Be Named Later.

The heroic instructor at Kentucky was indeed scheduled to teach the summer following the spring he caught those students, and again in the fall. Good for him. At least he has a modicum of job security—even if he does have to teach the exact same course over and over again.

For many contingent faculty, we teach the same course or courses in a cycle of underpaid, mind-numbing work that Sisyphus would run from. Well, maybe not Sisyphus, since he didn't have much of a choice—but neither do many contingent faculty.

Maybe Professor TBD has a full-time position, even. Fingers crossed. Professor Cain, if you're reading this, I'm rooting for you. However, it doesn't look like he has his own office, from this list of Stats instructors that I found. His title is "Staff Instructor of Statistics." And although he has an email address, unlike the rest of his cohort, he does not have an office address.

Except—from the story—he seems to have an office—the one that the students broke into. So that means that, although he does have an office (whether his own, or shared), no one at his institution has bothered to update the website with his information, which is completely normal when you are contingent. I was once told that because I was contingent, my name didn't need to be in the faculty directory because I was likely to be gone soon. The point is, Professor Cain's experience is not unique. His experience is normal, and normalized, across higher ed. But that doesn't mean it is okay.

But I haven't gotten to the best part of the story yet. The capstone. At the end of the story in the *Times*, the University of Kentucky spokesman Jay Blanton had this to say about the circumstances and his overworked, underpaid academic laborer: "'Cheating and theft of this kind is very serious in an academic institution,' he said, adding that episodes like this were rare at the university's College of Arts and Sciences, which has 10,000 students. 'It's an unusual set of circumstances,' he said. 'It also underscores how late our faculty work.'"

My God, Blanton. There's nothing to be proud of about how late Professor Cain was working. When your underpaid, overworked, contingent faculty are in the building at two o'clock in the morning, you should be ashamed, not proud. You should be asking what your institution is doing wrong that your faculty must work at two a.m. in order to get their work done on time. You need to figure out what you can do better so that they can have a reasonable quality of life. You don't brag about the long hours they work in the largest newspaper in the United States. Your bragging shows that the University of Kentucky is just like every other school I've worked at and researched: you don't care about the health and well being of your contingent faculty at all. Your professor may be a hero, but you have failed.

THIRTEEN

The Racism False Equivalence Strikes Again

In June 2017, Essex County College in New Jersey, a community college, fired a Black, non-tenure-track professor, Lisa Durden, because "officials say she made racially insensitive comments on Fox News." (That's what the Associated Press reported, with this headline: "NJ college: Professor fired for racially insensitive remarks.") Durden appeared on *Tucker Carlson Tonight* on June 6. Two weeks later she was out of a job.

Durden appeared on Tucker Carlson's show—and at this point, all I can think is that Durden must be a cool-headed woman to go anywhere near a person whose goal in life is to anger rational people and make them lose their cool—to talk about a Black Lives Matter Memorial Day celebration on her campus that was for Black people only.

Tucker, all fake-innocence, wanted to know why white people couldn't go, too, and isn't that racist to have an event for Black people only? He said, "I thought the whole point of Black Lives Matter was to speak out against singling out people based on race? ... Explain that to me."

Durden replied, "What I say to that is, 'Boo-hoo, you white people are angry because you couldn't use your white privilege card to get invited to the Black Lives Matter all-black Memorial

Day celebration.' Let me contextualize that for you." At that point in her reply, Tucker started talking over Durden, acting angry at her words.

Honestly, this far into in the conversation about Black Lives Matter, if there are white people who still cannot understand that the purpose of Black Lives Matter is not to "single out people based on race" but rather to point out how Black lives, you know, *matter*, then I don't know what to do. There are only two possible explanations for Tucker's question. Either he is very, very stupid. Or he was asking a specious question.

I think he was asking a specious question—a question in bad faith. Black Lives Matter is not about the cessation of singling people out. It's about the cessation of violence against Black bodies. Tucker knew that. His question was in bad faith, and it was intended to rile up his guest.

But none of that matters. At all. I don't have to explain how right-wing talk show hosts use rhetorical fallacies to frustrate conversation. That sort of wordplay is the bread-and-butter of Fox News and its brothers-in-arms.

The problem here is that a contingent faculty member stepped out of the ivory tower to engage in a public debate. She took a risk in appearing on a right-wing television show. And she lost her job for it.

Two days after the show aired, Essex County College fired Durden, right in the middle of the semester. Note that never once on the air did she mention that she was affiliated with the college. She made it clear that all of her views were her own.

But her taking care to maintain distance from the college didn't matter to Essex. Her hard work taking a stand as a public intellectual didn't either. They fired her anyway, and they did it, quite openly, because of her speech on Tucker's show. Here's an excerpt from the statement on her firing from Anthony Munroe, Essex County College President: "The character of this institution mandates that we embrace diversity, inclusion, and unity. Racism cannot be fought with more racism."

So now we have to talk about false equivalences (a common rhetorical fallacy), because we have one of the biggest of them all to deal with here: Tucker's "but I thought" nonsense and then this near direct quote of Supreme Court Justice Clarence Thomas by college president Munroe, "racism cannot be fought with more racism." Both Tucker and Munroe are saying the same thing: "reverse racism is the same as racism" or "racism by Black people is the same as racism by white people." Or however you want to frame it.

A false equivalence is a logical fallacy that happens you take two opposing viewpoints and claim they are equal—but they aren't. False equivalence is a favorite of people making racist arguments; it was the undergirding of "separate, but equal;" and it persists in racist arguments to this day.

"Reverse racism is equivalent to racism" is a false equivalence. It's one of the oldest, in fact. Here's the deal: Racism is the tidal wave of history, social influence, governmental control, violence, wealth, white supremacy, and everything else that gives white people—AS A GROUP—power over people of color—AS GROUPS. In individual interactions, racism plays out in individual ways, sure. But there can be no "reverse racism" until there has been, say, half a century or more of racial oppression of white people by Black people.

I can understand Tucker's nonsense because that is literally his schtick: to say offensive things to people who work hard to make the world a better place in order to provoke them. I have no idea how he sleeps at night. Who cares about Tucker. He's a clown.

But I cannot understand how a college president doesn't understand the most basic of logical fallacies. I presume he took freshman composition. I taught that course for a decade, and all of my students walked out of my class knowing how to spot a false equivalence.

But let's say rhetorical fallacies are not Munroe's strong suit. Fine. At the very least, as a college president, Munroe must understand intellectual freedom and the First Amendment.

Durden's situation is one of many reasons why I will never return to higher education, even when friends forward me promising jobs. We—all of us trying to make the world a better place—need to be able speak our minds, especially now. We can't be, even unconsciously, holding our tongues because we're afraid of getting fired, not if we have another option. Some of us, as Durden's experience has shown us, don't have another option. But some of us do, and it is our duty to carry that weight.

Unless you are a professor with tenure (and even then) higher education no longer cares about the duty of a professor to "profess"—from the Latin, which means to declare, publicly. Today's university wants automatons who will toe the line of a consumerist model and, most importantly, keep their mouths shut.

Durden wasn't fired because of reverse racism. She was fired because of plain old regular racism. She was a Black, female, non-tenure-track professor, the most vulnerable member of the professoriate, the most likely to be fired, the most contingent, the most likely to be criticized for being too loud or too disruptive. No one should be surprised that she lost her job. Higher education fails to protect people like her all the time.

But we should all be angry. And then we should take that anger, and we should do something about it. Use your platforms to call attention to stories like this. Stand up for your fellow faculty if you are still in the academy, and for faculty at the institutions where you are alumni. Whatever you do, if you are able to do so, do something.

FOURTEEN

What's Your BATNA?

IN ANY NEGOTIATION, BEING WILLING TO WALK AWAY MEANS THAT YOU essentially have all of the power. Sure, the other side might have some things that you wish you had, but in the end, if you don't agree to their terms, the side that most wanted the contract is the loser.

Here's an example. Most of us were taught, probably by a parent, that the first rule of car buying is to be willing to walk away from a deal you don't like. In my house growing up, walking away was not only the first rule of car buying, it was the first and the second rule of car buying. (Our third rule was to never use paint color as a decision factor.) Applying the walk-away rule to a car deal puts the power in your hands rather than the seller's. (That is a bit of an oversimplification. You might feel a little sad leaving the car behind. But you'll get over it knowing you did the right thing.)

Of course not all negotiations are so simple. Among the most difficult are the ones we do in the workplace. And job negotiations in the academic workplace are often especially fraught. For non-tenure-track employees of all stripes, our lack of leverage and job security often means that we have little negotiating power at all. If you are a contingent faculty member at a university without collective bargaining, how can you negotiate more favorable conditions?

BATNA: Best Alternative to a Negotiated Agreement

I don't have a magic answer for fixing the lack of leverage that contingent faculty face, but I have a concept I want to share that helped me with my own negotiations: BATNA. It stands for: "best alternative to a negotiated agreement." Thinking in terms of BATNA can make your life off the tenure track—or your transition out of academia—a little more well planned and enjoyable.

The concept of BATNA was first introduced by Roger Fisher and William Ury in their 1981 book on negotiation *Getting to Yes: Negotiating Agreement Without Giving In.*

Guhan Subramanian, writing for the *Harvard Program on Negotiation Blog* (August 2018) writes that BATNA "is among one of the many pieces of information negotiators seek when formulating dealmaking and negotiation strategies." To figure out your BATNA, ask this question: "If your current negotiation reaches an impasse, what's your best outside option?" ("What is BATNA? How to Find Your Best Alternative to a Negotiated Agreement").

BATNA is not synonymous with your "bottom line," which, according to negotiation expert David Venter, refers to the "worst possible outcome that a negotiator might accept." Bottom lines are terrible. You don't want to negotiate with your eye on the bottom line. You want the best alternative, not the worst. If you can't agree with your adversary, you want your BATNA.

The function of BATNA, Venter explains, is that "it prohibits a negotiator from accepting an unfavorable agreement or one that is not in their best interests because it provides a better option outside the negotiation" (emphasis added). BATNA is the open door that you can run through as soon as you see that your negotiations are going awry. It's your escape route, he says.

As Fisher and Ury write in *Getting to Yes*, "The reason you negotiate is to produce something better than the results you can obtain without negotiating. What are those results? What is that alternative? What is your BATNA—your Best Alternative To a Negotiated Agreement? That is the standard against which any proposed agreement should be measured."

As a contingent faculty member, you might not feel like you have many outside options. I get it; I really do. It didn't take long for me to figure out that a career off the tenure track was going to be uncertain at best. For my own piece of mind, I realized I needed to take steps to create backup plans and stopgaps. Over time, those stopgaps became a career. One textbook became five. One column became many. One editing client became a steady stream. One day, I realized I had an outside option. And as time went on, that outside option got better and better.

BATNA is one of my favorite acronyms, right up there with FUBAR and SMITF. In fact, when you find yourself in a FUBAR work situation that makes you want to SMITF, you need to consider your BATNA and then go talk to your boss.

Over the Barrel

What led me to think about BATNA? I spent eleven years as a non-tenure-track employee of various universities. My positions varied widely: I worked at three different universities, in four different divisions, in five different positions off of the tenure track teaching writing. Once, I had a job where I started out with a three-year contract. I thought it was going to be fantastic. Then the head of the division called all contingent faculty into a room together and told us that all future contracts would be year-to-year. No more multi-year stability.

We were upset. But there was nothing we could do. After all, a year-to-year job was better than no job, and most of us needed jobs. We had no leverage to demand longer contracts. If we all quit together (which would never have happened anyway, given the particular dynamics of our group), the division head could have replaced us with new people. We preferred to think that "new people" might not have been as good as we were, but who knows, really. There are many excellent unemployed professors out there.

The division chair had us over a barrel. Having no negotiating power was a terrible feeling.

A few weeks later, the division chair called us into that room again, and this time told us that not all of our contracts would be renewed the following year. Some of us would have to be cut. The administration, we were told, would be reviewing course evaluations to make the decision of who to keep and who to fire. (The word "fire" was never used, of course. I believe "not renewed" was the preferred euphemism.)

Once again, we were over a barrel.

At this point, I'd been working in the division for three years without a raise. And there were no raises—not even cost-of-living increases—on the horizon. Instead, we were playing a real-life game of *Survivor* in academe.

If you want to know why adjuncts and other non-tenure-track faculty unionize, just ask around for stories like that one. They're everywhere in the academy. Broken promises, gameshow-like competitions pitting employees against one another to retain their jobs. When my division chair announced this academic version of *Survivor*, I left that job without trying to negotiate. What would I have negotiated?

Luckily, I had a place to land: in another non-tenure-track job in another division at my same university, one with nother three-year contract. I thought things would be better. They weren't. There are some things that will always be problems so long as there are haves (tenure-track faculty) and have-nots (contingents). The tenure-track faculty got paid twice as much as we did to do the same (and sometimes less) work. They had special privileges we never saw. But the social interaction was the worst part: To the tenured faculty, our names weren't worth learning. We weren't worth knowing.

After three years in this new division, I put in for a promotion to the non-tenure-track equivalent of associate professor. I received the promotion. I did not receive a raise or any other added benefits. Just a new title. The division chair told me that that's just how it was. I couldn't expect anything better.

I was a mother of two, pushing 40, and tired of playing *Academic Survivor*. If I was so great that the division would promote me to associate, then it needed to give me a raise and a few other things, too. It was time to negotiate for real. And to do that, I needed leverage. I needed to figure out my best alternative to negotiated agreement—my BATNA.

Start Thinking About Your BATNA

If all you do after reading this chapter is start rethinking your work situation, then you're already on your way to conceptualizing your BATNA. Having a strong BATNA means shifting the power to your hands and out of the hands of those people who force you to play *Survivor* with your colleagues. It means that—if at any point you can't reach a fair negotiated agreement with your chair or dean—you have an alternative.

Often, as you can imagine, that alternative involves leaving your current position. But not always.

Creating your BATNA is the hard part. I was lucky. My first division—with its surprise contract changes—made me paranoid about job security. My paranoia made me feel like I needed to build up outside sources of income. So I start writing books and building up a consulting business—essentially, without really planning a career for it, I started freelancing on the side. And over the course of eight years, that unplanned freelancing work started to pay off.

As I became more aware of my tenuous job security, I worked

hard so my side-gigs would pay off. Then, when I got my final fake promotion, I had a strong BATNA. The strongest I could hope for, in fact: I was willing to leave the job if the division didn't meet my terms. And leaving wouldn't be a desperate move on my part. I would be leaving to do something that would make me just as happy as the job I'd been in. Leaving my job was truly a good alternative for me.

One other thing: BATNA relies on context. When you compare your academic job with your alternative career options, you might see—as I did—that your best alternative to negotiating more favorable working conditions inside academia is a strong job outside of academia. Or, you might find a new job at another campus, or in another division at your institution, and be able to use that new job as your BATNA.

My BATNA was my willingness to work as a freelance academic instead of an employee of the division that gave me the fake promotion.

But your current BATNA could be simply doing less in the job that you now hold: doing less unpaid service or holding only the minimum of office hours. All of the "adjunct heroics" (as Rebecca Schuman has put it) may need to go out the window. Then you'll have time for your own work that could lead to alternative income—like writing a book or consulting on the side. You'll have time to strengthen your BATNA now. After all, who knows when you might need it.[1]

FIFTEEN

Leaving a Legacy Off the Tenure Track

MANY CONTEMPORARY WRITERS ON PSYCHOLOGY—SPECIFICALLY THE psychologies of work, business, and economics—have written about the value of intrinsic motivation. First observed by researchers in the 1950s,[1] and built upon in the 1970s,[2] intrinsic motivation is often contrasted with extrinsic motivation. The latter is akin to "the carrot and the stick," while intrinsic motivation originates from internal drives to be good at things and to enjoy them—drives that seemingly have very little to do with carrots and sticks.

Graduate school is one long lesson in intrinsic motivation. No supervisor sits in your crappy apartment telling you to read and write, to stay late in the lab and conduct research after everyone else has left, or to prep for class after class. In other words, there is no stick. As far as carrots go, you don't get paid much (or at all) for the work you do in graduate school. You get little praise, especially in the short term. Viewed from the outside, you seem to be working, quite literally, for nothing.

All of which suggests you don't pursue a Ph.D. unless you are an intrinsically motivated person. Furthermore, students must significantly delay gratification while in graduate school, another quality of intrinsic motivation. The benefits (and negative consequences) of working (or not working) are a ways down the line—and nearly impossible to see if you are the kind of person who needs instant, external motivation to keep working.

So graduate students—in the United States, at least—are intrinsically motivated, delay gratification, and work for pennies. And here's the kicker: They do all of those things hoping for a tenure-track job that will likely never come—and, perhaps, was never meant to come.

As Kelly J. Baker pointed out in her 2016 *Chronicle Vitae* essay "Academic Waste," graduate students earning their Ph.D.s teach undergraduates on the cheap—a system that allows universities to continue to make their budgets. Writing about Marc Bousquet's 2008 book *How the University Works*, Baker notes, "New Ph.D. holders are not 'products' of our training, but 'byproducts' of academia. Graduate students and 'non-degreed flex workers' exist mostly to serve the university's labor demands. They generate cheap labor. Then they get replaced." If doctoral students and newly minted Ph.D.s aren't working toward the status of professor, a status that seems less and less likely to ever come, then what are they working for?

Agency, Mastery, and Legacy

People who write about business psychology agree that, in our current economy, fostering intrinsic motivation in workers creates the best outcomes for businesses. Some businesses (and business gurus) call that sort of motivation "happiness." Others focus on "culture" to foster motivation. But what keeps coming up again and again across all of the business psychology books and articles I've read (none of which I endorse, by the way) are three main concepts that work together as a coherent motivational theory: agency, mastery, and legacy.

I do, by the way, endorse the notion of agency, mastery, and legacy.

What do those words mean? According to Nathaniel Koloc's

2013 article in the *Harvard Business Review*, "Build a Career Worth Having" you can think of these three words like this.

Agency is the "ability to choose who you work with, what projects you work on, where and when you work each day, and getting paid enough to responsibly support the lifestyle that you want."

Mastery "refers to the art of getting better and better at skills and talents that you enjoy using, to the extent that they become intertwined with your identity."

Legacy is your "higher purpose." It is what you want to leave behind when you leave this world. It is your bigger picture. For an academic, perhaps your legacy is a book. Perhaps it is a documentary film. Perhaps it is a scholarly article that means something to you. Only you know what you want your legacy to be.

Typically, you have to have agency in order to acquire mastery. And you have to have mastery in order to leave a legacy. The concept of legacy helps explain why contingent faculty continue to publish and present on their research—even when the work isn't paid as part of their jobs or valued in any way by their academic institutions. Most non-tenure-track faculty never even have agency (let along mastery and legacy). They're given the same course to teach over and over, often a survey course outside of their expertise. They're often handed a pre-set syllabus and a standard textbook. The point is, there is often no creativity—no agency—to teaching as an adjunct, just repetitive 4-4 and 5-5 course loads, teaching the same introductory course, over and over, year in and year out.

And that lack of agency is a problem given how intrinsically motivated most faculty members are.

Off the Tenure Track Without Agency

Now, take a person who is so intrinsically motivated that she can earn a doctorate, and stick her in a repetitive, uncreative non-tenure-track job. She likely just graduated from a program in which she wrote an entire book on an entirely new idea that she invented out of thin air. She supported that idea with an immense amount of self-directed research, research she had to conduct in order to earn the credentials required for this job in the first place.

In her new job, she teaches four or five sections of the same introductory course each semester. The course uses a curriculum developed by the department, one that is standardized across sections, so she cannot deviate from the syllabus. She has no research support. Her "colleagues" barely know her name. She is on a year-to-year contract. She has no job security.

How can we expect her to thrive in this new environment?

The agency-mastery-legacy concept has really helped me understand one of the big reasons why contingent faculty end up hating their jobs so much that they quit for what may seem (to people still in the academy) like boring, non-life-of-the-mind work in the private sector. Ph.D.s leave academe in search of opportunities that provide—you guessed it—agency. Then mastery. And then, hopefully, legacy.

Finding Agency Within the System

But what if you don't want to leave academe? Or can't? Can non-tenure-track faculty find agency, mastery, and legacy while working within the adjunct academic system? How can you make your mark?

The first thing I can tell you is this: What you want your legacy to be is a very personal decision. But the second thing I can tell you is that academics are trained to believe that their academic legacy should be one very particular thing—a monograph, a grant, a discovery. For the longest time, for example, I believed that if I didn't publish a scholarly monograph that I had failed to achieve my professional legacy.

Why did I think that? Why? I have absolutely no use for a scholarly monograph (a book of research, usually published with a university press, that a professor writes for other professors to read). I have no time to write one, and it would make me no money—it would probably cost me money—and no job I would ever want would care if I had one. I've thought hard about the source of my belief, and the only thing I can come up with is academic brainwashing. Such brainwashing is a powerful thing— do not underestimate its influence. Once I finally set aside the monograph goal, I felt incredibly free.

You need to be sure that what you want to leave as your legacy is what you really want—not what you think you should want, or what "real" academics want, or what you are supposed to do in order to get a tenure-track job. (That's not a legacy, that's a résumé.)

In many ways, working off the tenure track gives you great freedom. If you don't want to write a monograph, you don't have to. Write something else instead: a memoir, a novel, a textbook, an oral history of some fascinating historical event. Then sell it and start earning some passive income. Maybe your legacy is the students whose lives you've touched. Wonderful. Figure out a way to focus on that—try to find agency, mastery, and legacy in your teaching.

Sit down and figure out what you want to leave behind in this world. Then figure out what kind of freedom—agency—you need in order to gain the skills—mastery—to be able to produce that kind of legacy.

You already have the intrinsic motivation. You just need to point it at something, and let it fly.[3]

SIXTEEN

Why Attend Conferences as a Freelance Academic?

FOR A FREELANCE ACADEMIC, ATTENDING A SCHOLARLY CONFERENCE can seem like a confusing proposition.

If you're an independent scholar—that is, someone who is unaffiliated with an institution but who chooses to continue to do research in a scholarly field—attending a conference makes sense. You want to stay apprised of new research, and present your own. I can understand that.

But what if you're a freelance academic, and you don't do scholarly research anymore? What if you have instead turned your research skills to generating freelance income? Scholarly conferences can seem pointless—you don't have much to offer them, and they don't seem to have much to offer you.

You're no longer on the job search, so you don't need that scholarly line on your C.V.

Plus, attending a conference without an institutional affiliation can feel alienating. Few really enjoy having "independent scholar" on their name tag. Or worse, a blank space under their name.

Plus, conferences are often expensive. The travel, the hotel, the conference fees, the food—you're looking at a thousand dollars, easy, and often more than that.

If you're not getting research support from an institution and you're not on the job hunt, conferences can seem like a colossal waste of time and money. And honestly, as a freelancer, what would you present on at a conference in your field? What could you possibly contribute?

The answer is: Far more than you might think.

For freelance academics who are considering attending an academic conference, here are some suggestions for how to overcome feelings of alienation and how to figure out what you have to contribute.

Alienation

Feelings of alienation, especially for those who have just recently left academia, might be the most difficult challenge to overcome on this front. You left the ivory tower. So why are you back on the academic-conference circuit? You don't have to earn tenure, so why are you presenting scholarship? What if the other conference attendees find out that you don't have an academic position? Isn't that kind of embarrassing?

Just because you aren't in an academic job doesn't mean you can't have a post within an academic organization. For example, I recently took a job as a mentor for a large scholarly organization; at its annual meeting the mentor program has its own gala, meet-and-greets, and other events. I'm involved in a way that isn't about teaching or research.

Kelly J. Baker, a post-academic journalist, editor, and author, wrote in *Chronicle Vitae* about attending her discipline's annual meeting as the chair of a task force on contingent faculty. In "What Can Learned Societies Do About Adjuncts?" she described how, although she wasn't an academic when she attended the conference, she had a purpose. Eventually, Baker left the task force, once it became apparent that her efforts weren't going to bring about change, but her efforts were still valuable—and your efforts can still be worth your time, even if you fall short of your goals.

Time and Money

It's true: Most conferences are very, very expensive. I would never suggest that you attend one for any reason if you can't afford it. Right at this moment I'm working on an accommodation for a member of a panel I'm chairing. She's disabled as well as strapped for cash. We're working out plans so that she can Skype rather than pay to travel across the country and spend money she does not have.

If you feel like a conference is going to be a waste of time and money, then trust your instincts. Don't go. Don't go just because you feel like you should. Don't go because you miss your old friends. Instead, visit them on your own time, when you can spend quality time together. Don't go because you feel like you're missing out on the zing of academia. Spending thousands of dollars on a conference isn't going to bring back the zing. It's just going to make you broke.

But there are reasons to go if you can afford it.

You can network with colleagues and clients. You can pitch a textbook to book editors. You can give a workshop on a topic, refine the workshop based on your experience, add that workshop to your résumé, and advertise similar workshops in the future, for money, because now you have experience leading such a workshop. Which leads me to my final suggestion.

What Do You Present?

Say you have decided to submit a proposal to present at the conference. What do you submit if you are no longer interested in the tenure treadmill? As a freelance academic, how can you make a conference presentation meaningful to your career outside of academia?

You can always present traditional scholarship, of course, even if tenure is not your goal. Scholarship has many benefits beyond earning you tenure. Presenting scholarship can help you establish an identity as an expert in a particular field—as someone who might be hired by those outside of the field as, say, a consultant. If you present on the latest developments in a particular area of sociology, think about how your work might translate to freelance writing or consulting. Always think about how you might double-dip.

Of course, you might present your scholarship simply because you enjoy it.

Workshops

But there are other ways to share knowledge at a scholarly conference that do not involve presenting traditional scholarship per se.

Do you lead workshops as a freelancer? I do. I teach people how to pitch their work to media outlets, for example, especially former academics. The first time I gave that workshop, though, was at a scholarly conference.

So here's my last piece of advice: Suggest a workshop in your area—say, as a roundtable—at your field's conference. For example, if you lead workshops on interviewing skills as a freelancer, the conference for your learned society might be interested in having you lead a workshop for graduate students on interviewing skills as well. The same goes for workshops on résumé writing, social-media best practices, and online portfolio design. Any skill that you teach outside of academia is a skill that workers who are still in academia would likely be interested in learning.

In short, bring your freelancer skills back into the academy via a scholarly conference. You'll be surprised, too, by how many people in your learned society will be interested in what you have to teach. [1]

SEVENTEEN

Why Am I Teaching Again?

You know that James Bond movie with the 52-year-old Sean Connery playing an aging Bond? The one with the tongue-in-cheek title, *Never Say Never Again*? Apparently, that title referred to a statement Connery made years before making the movie, in which Connery had said he'd never, ever, ever play Bond again. And yet there he was, up on the big screen, trying to get those nukes back from SPECTRE.

Over in 2014, I left teaching. I'd been working in a contingent, non-tenure-track job—one committee even referred to my particular job status as "untenurable." (That word is apparently a thing now.) I'd had enough, so I was out the door. Goodbye. Never again.

Then, in the winter of 2016, I received an email out of the blue from the continuing education department of a local university: Would I be interested in teaching a creative-writing course for them in the spring semester?

Would I? I had no idea.

Cons

Because I do not use my gut to make professional decisions, I made a list of pros and cons. And because I'm a glass two-thirds-empty kind of person, I started with the cons.

Pay: The pay for the course would be $125 for six weeks of teaching, or $25 a course meeting. I would have to teach one 90-minute class a week, plus there would be class-preparation time. Furthermore, on the payment paperwork, there was a sentence that read, "Many instructors choose to donate their honorarium to the [continuing education] program." Let me be clear: The university that asked me to teach for it was Duke University. Duke University was asking me to donate my teaching pay to Duke University. To be honest, sometimes I feel like my job as a higher education writer is to simply record reality for other people to read, no commentary necessary.

Location: The course meeting place was located far enough away from my home to constitute an "annoying" commute.

Coffee: The building where I would be teaching did not allow food or drink, which meant that even though my class would be in the morning, I wouldn't be allowed to bring coffee to class. Up until this class, I had literally never taught a class without a coffee mug in my hand.

Pros

But there were some pros to teaching this class. It turned out that I wasn't going to be an underpaid, coffee-deprived ghoul for no reason at all.

Course content: I would be teaching a creative-writing workshop—in particular, narrative writing, my favorite. I would have complete control over my curriculum, including how many pages my students turned in each week to workshop.

Class size: I could limit the course to eight students. In fact, I could have made it smaller, but eight seemed like a good size to me. If I chose to teach the course in the future, I could have six students, or even fewer.

Class frequency: The course only met once a week, which seemed very doable. I have never, ever taught a once-a-week course before. I wondered: What would that be like? Such a luxury! Such an extravagance!

Intangibles: The course would be a way to dip my toe into teaching a creative-writing workshop beyond the one-day workshops I'd done here and there in the past. Teaching creative writing for a university would give me credibility. The course would only be six weeks long, and let's face it, I can do anything for six weeks.

————

TEACHING THE COURSE SUDDENLY SEEMED LIKE ONE OF THOSE TIMES when exposure could actually be a good thing. And you'd better believe I took that $125 check. (Donate it? Were they serious?)

So I assigned *Bird by Bird* by Anne Lamott (of course) and headed off to teach my first "real" creative-writing workshop. And it was fantastic. The students were so eager to do the work, and had such great insights. I was so energized after class.

I remembered I loved teaching.

Holy crap. I love teaching.

It turns out that teaching on three campuses in two different cities while pregnant with my first child just to make a living wage wasn't able to beat my love of teaching out of me. The callous disregard of some of my so-called colleagues didn't, either.

I'd really thought my love of teaching had been tortured, beaten, murdered, and buried. I'd imagined my love of teaching's tombstone: *Here lies Katie's love of teaching. It lived for 20 years, starting when she taught kiddos to swim as a teen. Killed by a four-four course load, freeway flying, and jerks.*

But no. I still love it. These eight creative writers of wildly different life experiences and skill levels reminded me why. Plus, I learned how to sneak a spill-proof coffee mug into my classroom.

But it wasn't just the students who reminded me why teaching is wonderful. Every one of the pros on my pro-con list helped, too. I had control over my course—its content, its size, its curriculum. For nearly a decade, I'd been handed a syllabus and a book and told what to teach. My own creativity could only fit in at the margins of a teaching career like that. Yes—core courses need be taught. But even in core courses, teachers can, and should, have some agency. (See Chapter 15 to learn more about agency and contingent faculty.) Too many departments, however, don't trust adjuncts. They don't allow them autonomy in their own classrooms. That's part of the problem with higher education today, and one of the reasons I left.

The best part about this course I taught was the relationship I formed with each of my students. Like you're supposed to do when you're teaching, I learned from them as much as they learned from me. They taught me about writing, about teaching writing, about all of the things that I want to be better at. I might have once said never again to teaching, but teaching again has brought me new friends, ideas, and fellow writers. And freelance academics need all the friends we can get.[1]

Practical Advice

EIGHTEEN

Launch Your Career Like James Bond

THIS CHAPTER, AND ALL OF PART III OF *THE FREELANCE ACADEMIC*, IS for all of the aspiring freelance academics out there, especially those who have absolutely no idea how to get started with a new career. You might still be in the academy, but you want to start dipping your toes in the pool of new, creative work outside of academia. Or, you might be ready to jump in head first. Either way, you might feel like you don't know how to become something other than an academic.

I understand, I really do. We were trained to be one thing. It's time to be something else. But that's easier said than done. Luckily, we have good role models.

I'm talking about James Bond.

Have you ever seen *Dr. No*, the very first James Bond movie? It's a good movie, as the old Sean Connery Bond flicks go. But what is most remarkable about the movie, to me, is this.

After the opening sequence in which a British operative in Jamaica is assassinated, the film cuts to London, to an exclusive gaming club called Les Ambassadeurs. (Note: it still exists.) A man enters the club, and at the door, the maître d' stops him and asks if he is a member. The man pulls out his card and hands it over, saying he is looking for a person called James Bond.

If you were watching this movie upon its release in 1962, this moment would be the first time in cinematic history you would have ever heard that name.

The film cuts to a woman in a red evening gown playing a card game called "chemin-de-fer" (a version of baccarat), and she is losing against the player dealing the cards. When she calls for more chips from the bank, the voice of the unseen dealer finally speaks to her.

"I admire your courage, Miss..."

"Trench, Sylvia Trench. And I admire your luck, Mr. ..."

"Bond, James Bond." That's the first time we hear those words spoken by the man. The first time we hear his voice.

And shortly after, for the first time, we see his face. And at that moment, we hear the low, thrumming guitar score that for the past 55 years we've come to associate with James Bond.

But remember: In 1962, you'd never heard that song before. You'd never heard him introduce himself before. You didn't know who he was.

But none of that matters. When you watch *Dr. No* today, you wouldn't know if it were the first Bond movie or the 10th. Watching that movie, it feels like James Bond has always been James Bond—that James Bond has always existed. That he's always been wooing the Sylvia Trenches of the world at 3 a.m. at exclusive casinos in Mayfair, that he's always been sent dashing off to confront SPECTRE in Jamaica.

My God, he's so Bond in *Dr. No* it's nearly unbearable. Because he says his name in such a way, in such a tux, in such a place that he expects you, his audience, *to already know who he is.*

Bond magically appears fully formed, like Athena springing from the head of Zeus. At least at the beginning of the Bond franchise, there was no birth of Bond, no origin story.

So what does *Dr. No* have to do with your freelance career?

I coach new writers a lot. They are often transitioning from other careers. I get asked questions like, "I don't have a lot of clips or publications—what would I put on a website?" Or,

"How do I write a social media profile, when I'm basically a nobody?"

The best advice I can give is to take a page from James Bond in *Dr. No*.

You are right now, starting today, a public figure. You are, starting today, a writer, or an editor, or a consultant, or a coach. Whatever freelance career path you have chosen to take, you are, right now, already on that path. You need to simply decide that you are what you are, that your creative work is why you are, and then make sure that every public document you put out there reflects that decision.

How do you make this happen?

Let's use writing as an example. If you're looking to start a freelance writing career, chances are you'd be surprised how much writing you've actually done. If you are a person who loves writing, you've probably written more than you think. What "counts" as writing is a bigger net than you think. What kinds of writing did you do for your academic job? Think beyond just your conference papers and journal articles. What about grants? Proposals? Slide-decks? Reports for committees? Those count, too. Put a bullet point on your website about your experience with grant writing or professional writing. You can make a lot of money helping businesses with their high-stakes business writing.

Second, when you create your freelance writer website, take into account all of the things that you are. Don't limit yourself to just one narrow band of interest. You will have plenty to put on your website. But the most important thing is to launch your website as though it were a website that had always been there, professional in appearance, representing you, the professional. Never say that your site is "in progress." If you have a page that isn't finished, leave it down until it is. Never have a page say "under construction." Each web page—your entire site—will appear online fully formed and professional. (Even if, in your mind, there is always more you can add. The world doesn't need to know that.)

Bond, James Bond. Dot com.

The same goes for your social media profiles—all of them. Yes, you need those, too. You are going to burst onto the public scene like Athena. You will not apologize. You will not be "beta" or "just figuring this thing out." You will be a pro from the get-go. Or, at least you will fake like you are until you are. You want to inspire confidence in other people. And you want to inspire confidence in yourself.

Look like a professional, until one day, you are a professional. And then you'll see that there's not much difference, in the end.

NINETEEN

How to Start Working for Yourself

In 2014, when I quit my job as a non-tenure-track professor to work as a full-time freelancer, I had no idea what I was doing. I've been lucky, and so far, I've made a pretty good run of it. I want you to have more than luck on your side. That's one of the reasons I wrote this book.

If you're looking for advice on how to do what I've done, there's a lot of it out there, including other chapters in *The Freelance Academic*. Some of the advice I've written is meant to help you figure out your new relationship with your old career—that is, with academia. I wrote that advice because figuring out how to separate from higher education isn't easy.

And some of the advice I've written is more practical, especially the advice in Part III of this book. Here, in Part III, is the advice (at least some of it) that you will need day-to-day as you embark on your freelance academic career.

Getting Started

There are a few things that you need to know right out of the gate if you are going to start working for yourself. The goal of this chapter is to tell you a couple of things I've learned from doing what I do. What I do is consulting, writing, and editing. My advice might not apply to you, if you don't do what I do. But if your work is similar, then you might find some things here that will help.

The first thing you need to know is this: Your academic training has definitely prepared you to make a living outside of academia. This fact is incontrovertible, despite anything you might have experienced in graduate school or what you might read in the popular media about how academics are useless. We're not useless. And we make good livings outside of academia all the time. The evidence supporting this claim is sound.

Here's the second thing you need to know: Your academic training has likely not prepared you to work for yourself. It has not prepared you to run a business.

What do these two things mean, together? If you want to leave academia and work in the private sector, in the public sector, or for some hybrid thereof, you are prepared to do so. Study up on how to transition, and do it. (There's a reading list in the back of this book with resources.)

But if you want to leave academia and work for yourself, you're going to have to learn how to work as a freelancer and likely also as a small business owner. And, as the title of this book suggests, freelancing is what I'm here to talk about.

Sometimes Freelancing Isn't a Choice

Let's take a step back and appreciate that a lot of us didn't take up freelance careers because we wanted to. We did it because we had to. What is now called "the gig economy" has been forced upon workers just as contingency has been forced upon higher education. Businesses have cut back on full-time employees and replaced them with independent contractors (freelancers) who receive paychecks but no benefits. Because the businesses don't have to pay benefits, worker's compensation insurance, or FICA taxes (Medicare or Social Security), these "1099" employees save the businesses a lot of money.

A lot of workers have had no choice but to turn to freelancing. They've lost their jobs, and the only way to keep working in their fields is to sell their services to various companies—often the same companies these people used to work for as W-2 employees. As independent contractors, they often make less money than they used to as full timers, and of course they have little or no job security.

Not only do freelancers have to purchase their own health insurance, they have to hustle for every job. Despite the positive spin that freelance-heavy companies that Uber have put on the word, "hustling" for a living isn't pleasant. Then, after a freelancer has hustled to get a job, and done the work, she might get stiffed by her client, and with little recourse. According to a 2016 article in *Fast Company*, citing a survey by the Freelancer's Union (freelancersunion.org), half of freelancers reported getting cheated by a client in 2014. Furthermore, the "average amount lost was $6,390. For the average respondent, that amount represented 13 percent of their annual income" (Sara Horowitz, "Why Freelancers Need A Nonpayment Law"). The problem is, freelancers have a hard time collecting that lost money. W-2 employees wouldn't have such a hard time: "If this were to happen to a full-time employee, they would be entitled to file a wage-theft complaint with the Department of Labor." The Freelancer's Union is working on a campaign to get bills passed at the state level to protect against freelance wage theft.

In many ways, contingency is the gig economy of higher ed. So why move from one gig economy to another? If both careers—working off the tenure track and working as a freelance academic —are so similar, why not stick with what we know, with contingency in academia? Because in practice, they're not so similar at all. In my job, I call the shots. I don't wait around hoping my contract is renewed. I don't have to put up with colleagues—clients—who treat me poorly. Ever. But at the same time, the "gig" economy can be tough. Freelancing requires you to think about money in a vastly different way. You will probably need to pay yourself a steady paycheck, for example, even though some months you'll make less money than other months. You will probably need to consider incorporating or forming an LLC. (See Chapter 22, "Run Your Writing Like a Business," for more on business formations even if you're not a writer.) These important decisions, ones you never needed to think about when you worked for a university, and ones you don't need to think about if you choose to work for a company outside of academe.

But if you are going to work for yourself, you need to think about them now.

And if the uncertainty of a freelance career is too hard to take, then you shouldn't freelance. Get a more stable job. They're out there, and you're prepared for them. Best of all, they're more fulfilling than you likely think they are. It's not all *Office Space*. I promise.

I'm not here to burst any bubbles. I'm not here to say, "It's uphill both ways, whippersnapper." (I detest those people.) But anyone who knows me knows that I'm super practical. That's what this chapter is for: some practicality to mix into your planning.

Exploitation Ends Now

My first piece of advice to you is this: never (rarely) work for free.

I say "never work for free" because I'm a writer who writes for a living. I pay my mortgage with writing. I turn words into cash and buy food, diapers, and gasoline with that cash. But all of the time I'm approached by others and asked to do work for free. Sometimes, these are positive, well-meaning organizations who cannot afford to pay me. Other times, these are wealthy organizations (like universities with large endowments) who can.

As I explained in the introduction to this book, I have a theory about writing for free that guides my decision-making: There are a lot of great magazines out there that editors run for nothing. Sometimes, the magazines even lose money. These magazines publish stories that will make the world a better place. I write for magazines like that a lot. But if a magazine can afford to pay and it doesn't? That's exploitation. If it can afford to pay well, and pays poorly? Same.

Don't allow yourself to be exploited.

You can substitute a variety of verbs for "write." You know what skills you have that people pay other people for. You might be an editor. You might be a researcher. You might be a tutor, a website designer, a teacher, or a theatrical scenic designer. If you want to work for yourself, either part-time or full-time, the first step is learning how to ask people to pay you a fair wage for your work. And asking people to pay you for your work can be very hard when you are accustomed to getting a paycheck from a large institution (even a small paycheck).

In order to run your own business, you first have to value what you do. You have to value yourself. You do not edit, research, tutor, teach, or design in a way that exploits you. And you will know when you are being exploited. It doesn't feel good. You feel undervalued. It hurts inside, even just a little.

Your job, starting today, is to value what you're worth. What you're really worth. You need to do some research. Do you know how to do research? You bet you know how to do research. Find out what the going rates are in the private sector for what you do. Think about the rates that you should be charging, and start charging those rates. And remember, when you set your rates, you have to add 30% to what you think a fair hourly wage will be —because from now on, you are paying all of your taxes. No employer is picking up half of your Medicare and social security. Freelancers pay it all. Plus, you have to account for all of the time that you spend quoting jobs that don't happen.

If you're a new freelancer, I can tell you right now that your hourly rate is too low. It just is. Go raise it.

Remember how you used to have a C.V.? You don't have one

of those anymore. I used to have a C.V. too. When I had a C.V., and an academic career to go with it, I used to give talks for free. Conference presentations, invited lectures, lectures on my campus. Free, free, free. And then I quit my professorship. Now when people ask me to give a talk, they have to pay me to do it. They can't convince me to give with the "this will look great on your C.V." line. Because I no longer have a C.V. Now, I have a checking account into which I put money.

For example: soon after I started freelancing, the very university at which I used to work invited me to give a two-hour talk on my area of specialty to a group of professors—a professional-development seminar. I charged what I considered to be a vast amount of money. They agreed to my fee without hesitation.

Before I presented my fee proposal, I figured out how much to charge by asking around. The first thing I asked, in fact, was for "sample proposals" from the client for "prior lectures," and they sent me the proposals. I looked at the prices these other groups charged, and I charged similar prices. In other words, I educated myself about the going rate.

Full disclosure: there was a moment when I felt uncertainty. I asked myself terrible questions: Am I worth the going rate? Why me? Is this something that I'm worth being paid this much money to do? Call it self-doubt or imposter syndrome or whatever, I felt it, and I felt it hard.

And then I sent the proposal. And then, a few weeks later, I cashed the check.

Now I give talks at universities frequently. I charge plenty—I charge enough. This is my job, my livelihood. I keep a photograph of my kids on my desk because they're cute, sure. But I also do it to remind me that every hour I'm away from them on a far-flung campus must be worth it financially.

If you want to avoid being exploited and make sure you earn enough money to live on, you have to research, quote your work accurately, and bluff a little bit when you feel like maybe you aren't worth the rate you are quoting. But you are worth it. You have years of training, experience, expertise—in other words, you are an expert.

Figure out what you're worth. Quote accurately. Invoice. And get paid for your work.[1]

TWENTY

How Can You Earn Money?

When I started my first university job after graduate school, I lasted about half a year before I started a side-gig. While working as a lecturer, I wrote and sold a nonfiction book in my area of expertise to a publisher. The book wasn't anything fancy—I just put together all my teaching materials from a course I'd created, packaged them up for a pre-existing book series the publisher already had, wrote a proposal, and sent it off.

But I still get royalties from that book today, nearly ten years later.

More importantly, writing that book helped me land my next nonfiction book project and some speaking gigs. Because I'd written a book in an area that people in my field were interested in, more jobs came my way. Pretty soon, I had three reliable income streams: my main job, my book royalties, and my speaking engagements.

I kept writing, until one day I realized I didn't need the main job anymore. The side-gigs had become my main gigs.

After leaving full-time employment, it became even more important to think about the variety of income streams that could help me earn a living. Sure, I might think of myself as a "writer," but writing encompasses so much more than book royalties. Now I work as an editor, a freelance journalist, a writing coach, a copywriter and designer for websites, and, of course, an author. Each one of those income streams is valuable.

When I wrote that first book, I wasn't planning on leaving my job. At the time, I was happy doing what I was doing. But I did feel that having more than one source of cash was a way to financial stability. A table with one leg, or even two legs, isn't as stable as a table with four. When it turned out that my non-tenure-track job wasn't nearly as stable as I thought it was, I was very glad to have created the other sources of income.

So how do you get multiple income streams? Especially while working a regular job?

What Will People Pay You For?

The first step is figuring out what you are really, really good at. What are you better at than others around you? These are your superpowers. Superpowers can be small—say you're really good at organizing stuff. Or you're great with kids, like, you're the kid-whisperer. Maybe you're great at organizing stuff and you're the kid-whisperer, in which case you need to call me, and I will hire you.

Start making a list of your superpowers. Note: now is not the time to be modest. Now is the time to be the opposite of modest. Now is the time to act like you are your mom bragging about you to her friends and making you want to hide in the closet with embarrassment.

Once you have your list of superpowers, the hard part begins —because not every superpower can be turned into money.

Although these days, it seems nearly everything can.

Right now, though, we're looking for the low-hanging, monetizable fruit. If you're the person who is super good at organizing stuff, put an ad out on your neighborhood listserv offering your services. The thing to know is this: you only need one satisfied client. After you get one satisfied client, you can and will ask for a glowing testimonial. You will put that testimonial on a Facebook business page (you will have created a Facebook business page for your business) and on your website (you will have also created one of those), and you will get more clients. You give out that client's name as a reference. Business will snowball from there.

The first client is always the hardest.

Here are some other ideas:

Create a community. Start an organization blog, and befriend other bloggers who write about organizing stuff. They're out there. They're always out there.

Put tips on your business Facebook page—but put them out as graphical memes, with your business website at the bottom, so when they're shared, your business is shared, too.

Write a short ebook and sell it for a dollar—or give it away for free.

In short: become the expert that people want turn to.

Don't Wear Yourself Out

A side-gig does two things for you: it provides a financial safety net, and it provides a creative outlet. Let's talk about each of these things.

Say your organizing business side-gig has grown successful. You have a successful blog where you bring in advertising revenue and new clients. People pay you to write guest articles on major websites. You have clients all around town who pay you good money per hour to teach them how to make their homes more livable and how to make their businesses look cool. Your small business is successful. And you did it all while holding down your main job, too.

Why did you do all of this extra work? To buy a bigger television? If so, please do not tell me because I will be deeply disappointed in you. The whole point of this extra work is to create financial security—remember the table with lots of legs? You did not do this extra work to be able to see the manicured stubble on Tom Brady's chin at thirty paces.

Take the extra money you earn and pay off debt—student loans, car loans, credit card loans, all of it. Once the debt is paid off, save an emergency fund. Once your emergency fund is created, start saving for retirement. Eventually, once your debt is paid off and you have an emergency fund, you might be able to quit your main job.

If quitting your main job sounds like a dream, I can tell you that it isn't. I can tell you that it is, indeed, easier to do so if you are in a stable relationship with another adult who also has an income. It's also easier if you don't have children. But you can do it. In order to do so, you have to put your side-gig cash to good use. You have to relieve financial strain rather than creating more.

On the other hand, if you blow your side-gig money on stupid stuff, you'll simply create a spending pattern that you won't be able to maintain. One day, you'll realize that your side-gig has become a second, necessary, main gig, one that you won't be able to keep up with.

You will wear yourself out because you will be working two full-time jobs to maintain your new standard of living.

In short, don't buy a bigger television.

In the end, *The Freelance Academic* is about creativity—too many times our creativity is stifled by the work we have to do to pay the bills, leaving us too little time to do the work we want to do to feed our souls. That's what you're aiming for. That soul-feeding work.

One day, you might find yourself so enamored with your side-gig that you want to make it your main gig. Don't dig yourself a financial hole with the extra money from your side-gig. Start creating the financial freedom that you need to one day leave your job and turn your creative, fun, entrepreneurial work into your main work.

The multiple income streams with your new main gig—blogging, consulting, speaking, ebook sales, literally anything people will pay you to do—all centered around your superpower, are ways to express yourself creatively.

That's how you work as a freelance academic.

TWENTY-ONE

So You Want to Be a Freelance Writer

A LOT OF FREELANCE ACADEMICS, ESPECIALLY THOSE IN THE humanities and social sciences, want to make at least some of their money from freelance writing. That's great—as I wrote in Part I of this book, writing for the public is an important part of being a freelance academic. But the nuts-and-bolts of how to do so can be more complicated than people think when they first get started.

When I quit my full-time academic job to write for a living, the first thing I did was take an online course through a small company called The Thinking Writer. The course, called "How To Pitch and Submit," was taught by then-freelance writer Claire McGuire—and it changed my life. I needed to learn how to write freelance pieces that pay actual money. I did learn how to pitch articles and interact with editors. But the course taught me so much more than the genre of the freelance story pitch.

As I worked to make a career as a freelance writer, I came to learn that you can't actually feed your family on the bagels that online venues pay for your pieces. *The Chronicle of Higher Education* pays $300 per piece. Magazines like *Slate* and *The Atlantic* pay even less, like $100. Information on how much magazines pay freelance writers is crowd-sourced and public.

Check it out at the website *Who Pays Writers?* (whopayswriters.com). You'll see I mean. Bagels.

One particularly valuable component of the course consisted of interviews with freelance writers in which they described how they actually made a living. The interviewees, in an anonymous fashion, listed where their money came from each month. Their lists weren't sexy, but they were real, and they made me feel so much better about my chances of actually making it. The interviewees also provided really practical tips about how to make your money work as a freelance writer, when pay might be downright unpredictable. (For more on handling unpredictability, see Chapter 26, "Finding Stability as a Freelance Academic.")

So I'm here to tell you that you can make a living as a writer, but you (might) have to let go of some notions of what "making a living as a writer" means.

Where Does the Money Come From?

Just like those freelance writers did in that course I took all those years ago, I'm going to tell you where my money comes from.

- I publish 2-3 pieces in online magazines each month. I earn between four and six hundred dollars a month doing this. I used to publish more magazine articles each month, but pitching is a lot of work for the money, and I can make more money per hour doing other things.
- I have published four textbooks: two in English (my doctorate area) and two in law (my other degree area). These textbooks earn me royalties every year. The royalties are unpredictable on all of the books except for one. This one textbook earns me a lot of money every year. One day, it may stop earning me a lot of money. But for now, it does, and we (my husband and I) are figuring out a way to ensure that we save enough of

that income now (instead of buying more stuff) so that I can continue to have money to write more books in the future.

- I have published, including this book, two trade nonfiction books. "Trade" means books for a general audience. These books are reviewed well, but they aren't big sellers. They sell similarly to academic books. My biggest sales happen when universities adopt them for courses or for campus reading groups, or when I give talks at host universities.

- I have published three full-length novels and three novellas. The income from these is small, a few thousand dollars a year right now. When I tell people that number, they gasp. "But you're an Amazon bestseller!" or "Why do it then?" Answer to the first question: being a "bestseller" is a funny thing these days—it's true that thousands and thousands of people have my book now, and that's important to me. But selling lots of copies doesn't translate into lots of money, strangely enough. Answer to the second question: I write novels because I love it. If someone handed me two thousand dollars and said, "Go write a novel," that would be worth it to me. You have to know what is worth it to you.

- I am a developmental editor and writing coach. My clients, hilariously, make far more money selling their books than I do—often because my clients are already big-time novelists. Most of this work comes to me via referral. I helped one novelist a while ago, and then she told someone else, and the work snowballed from there. I also help academics who are struggling to turn their really interesting doctoral research into compelling books. Earlier I was talking about knowing your strengths—that's one of mine. I make good money doing this work. The best part is, I can invoice universities directly when I help writers who are employed by universities. (I never mind at all when I invoice universities.)

How much of what I just described is freelance writing for magazines? Not a lot. Writing for magazines is a lot of work. But it's very visible work, especially when a piece goes viral on social media. But when it comes to how many hours a day I spend writing those pieces, and worse, how much money they earn me, freelance journalism is a terrible way to make a living. But it is a good way to earn some money as part of your overall career, and it can lead to other work, like speaking jobs and book deals. Jennifer Polk, a smart and generous academic career coach, has a word for the type of career I have: a "portfolio career."[1] She writes, "A concept I come back to, time and again, is that there is no one right career. There is not one lone job title that's the key to meaningful work for you. You have multiple skills, interests, values and quirks that you could (and likely will) bring to bear in multiple lines of work." And that's okay.

For me, going forward, I see my work this way: First, I will continue to publish articles in magazines, but I'm writing more essays than researched or reported pieces, because essays are what I enjoy writing. Second, I will continue to work on my new editions of textbooks, when required. Third, I will continue to do editing work—because it's a solid income, and working with clients is satisfying—it's a lot like teaching. I will continue to write trade nonfiction and novels.

I am a novelist. I am a freelance writer. I am an editor. These identities are not mutually exclusive. In fact, the opposite is true. They are symbiotic.

The Transition from Academic Writer to Freelance Writer

We all have different talents that we can share with the world. The first step is figuring out what yours are—and what yours are not.

For example, I am a terrible, horrible, no good, and very bad copyeditor. My copyediting skills are literally the worst. When I do developmental editing, in my proposals, I specifically state that the services I will be providing do not include copyediting. But copyediting might be your jam. Start networking. Get copyediting work.

Say you are excellent at assessing websites. Like, you go to a website and in five seconds you can tell not only why it is terrible but how it could be better. The fonts make your eyes bleed. The words are a mess. You have some sort of mastery of web design and content that is a gift. Guess what? You are now a freelance writer who specializes in web content. Go figure out how freelance web content writers/designers get work.

Go make a living as a freelance writer.

But what if you want to be a freelance journalist? You want to write 1400 words for $150 on a 48-hour deadline? Okay, let's talk about that.

In my first novel, Entanglement, which came out in 2015, the hero (Timmy) and heroine (Greta) end up working together in a niche company owned by the hero, called Pacific Production Lighting. Pac Lighting owns hundreds of stage lights, thousands of meters of cable, multiple lighting control boards, hundreds of meters of truss (along with the chain motors to hang the truss from event spaces), and more. When Greta, the heroine, first enters Pac Lighting's warehouse, she's awestruck by the huge space and the huge amount of strange gear.

At readings, audience members often asked me how on earth I know so much about such a unique business. I seem to know an awful lot about the lights and cables and such. Did I just do a lot of research? The answer: Sort of. My husband owns a company very similar to Timmy's, which he formed when he graduated from college.

To create Timmy's company, I just used a preexisting database in my head (and in my husband's head), put the company on the West Coast instead the East Coast, and voilà, Pac Lighting was born. That's how you use your expertise in your writing. (Although researching new stuff is really fun, too.)

If you're an author, you already know about using your expertise in your writing. If you're an academic, you already know something about having an area of expertise and writing about it (with a boost from new research).

Both of those kinds of writing—writing novels and writing academic journal articles—take a long time. To write freelance articles for online venues, you need to consider your skills as a researcher and writer, and then speed them up. Way, way up. When you're talking about freelance journalism, you're talking about zippy work, and I mean fast-paced, dizzying work. The feedback, and the money, come quickly.

You're going to need to let go of some of those things that made you a good academic writer: the desire to research until you knew everything there is to know—you just won't have time for that anymore. The desire to avoid pissing anyone off in your field. You're going to piss off a lot of people, now. The desire to hedge, and then to hedge your hedges. Now, you're going to have plant your flag on a hill and defend it.

You're going to need to know your beats. You're going to need connections with editors who get you, who get your skills, and who get your quirks. You're going to need to know how to write a pitch. You're going to need to make good friends with deadlines.

Here are some ideas to get you started.

Turn Your Expertise into Your Beats

I'm going to go out on a skinny limb and guess that, as an academic, you have areas that you are super knowledgeable about. You have vast amounts of information in your brain about niche subjects. That's because everyone has something that she is really geeky about. And also because that's what it means to be an academic. If you're lucky, you have more than one area of expertise. And if you're even luckier, you have a hobby, too, that you know a lot about. These areas are about to become your beats.

In journalism, a "beat" is an area that you have in-depth expertise in. An editor might ask you, "What are your beats?" And, if you were me, you'd reply, "Higher ed, disability, mental health, sexual assault, and first amendment issues." I didn't start out with all of those beats. They grew as I worked more.

So how did I start? I started by writing a column on mental health and disability in higher education for an arm of *The Chronicle of Higher Education* called *Chronicle Vitae*. The more I wrote this column, the more I learned about the subject. The more of an expert I became.

But I was already an expert before I started because disability studies was one of my research areas. I took my main area of research, added a whopping dose of personal experience, and a column was born.

So, to find your beats, start by making a list of the things that you are an expert in. What are your areas of research, and how might these translate to something you can write about today? Here are some questions to get you started:

1. What are you an expert in?
2. What do you do for fun?
3. What could you write about as an expert with little extra work on your part?

I added the third one as a way to get you started. You might expand your beats with more research as you go, but as you begin, you want to find your easiest way in.

As you jot down your areas of expertise, start adding possible topics that you might want to write about. These are areas that you might have researched recently to solve a problem in your own life, or areas that you wish you knew more about. Tie your areas of expertise to current events. (Take a look at Chapter 3, "On

Writing," for more on the idea of using your current research as material for freelance pitches.)

After you make your list of expertise and possible topics, you need to figure out who would be interested in reading what you have to say about these areas. What magazines run pieces about your topics? What's trending, right now? Are any of your ideas "evergreen"—journalism-speak for always on trend? Or are some of them more urgent than others—are they "timely"? You need to find your targets, and then pitch them your timely pitches "pegged" to the current event.

Find Your Targets

When you were working as an academic, what venues did you like to read? (Please, don't say *The New Yorker*.) I'm talking about magazines that are online, niche, interesting—and where you found stories that seemed like stories you thought you might be able to write. That's where you should be pitching.

Think about the stories you want to write, read the magazines where you think you might see them in print, and then make a list. I use a spreadsheet software for this list because I also keep track of editors' names and their email addresses. But note: editorial staff change frequently, so always double-check before you send a pitch. I also keep track of the last time I pitched or published a story with that publication. But a simple list will do to get you started.

Don't forget to look at trade magazines. These pay well, by the way. A general rule of thumb: the less high profile a venue is, the more it pays freelancers. Trade magazines for medical supply devices pay really, really well. But no one you want to see your byline will see it. Your piece will never trend on social media. But if you want to make a living as a writer, make friends with trade magazines. Do you keep a backyard chicken coop? If you recently had to help your heirloom chickens through some health problems with the aid of your veterinarian, you could pitch a story to a veterinary or local farming trade magazine.

Then there are company websites. You could look for in-house blogger or copywriter jobs. Mostly, I get my professional writing jobs through networking, and through closed Facebook groups for people who do the work I do. You need to let people know what you are an expert in. That means you need a website, and you need to pitch stories.

Once you've compiled your list of targets to go with your areas of expertise, it's time for the next step.

Find Your Angles

An "angle" is a new thing to say about something old. "Higher education exploits adjuncts" is old news. A new angle would be something like, "Some universities are asking adjuncts to work for free, taking exploitation to new lows." This is a real thing, by the way. For example, see John Warner's piece in *Inside Higher Education*, "Volunteer Faculty: The Death Knell for Public Higher Ed," published April 25, 2018.

As a freelance writer, your job is to find new things to say about your areas of expertise and to pitch those things as stories to editors. The only way to know what other people are already saying is to read what's out there. Once you've read what's out there, you can figure out new things to say—that is, new angles.

After you've done your research in an area, start brainstorming story ideas. Really let your brain go free. Write down every crazy idea for a story that comes to your head. You want to have ten so you can pick the best one.

But you might end up publishing all ten, so don't lose track of them.

After all, if you sell one story, then write it, and then publish it (in a matter of days—it's usually a matter of days), you can turn around and sell an updated version of the story, with new information, building on that first story, the following week.

Writing on the same topic isn't wrong—it's called "having a beat." In fact, you put that earlier publication in your pitch (that's called a "clip") to show that you know what you're doing, and editors are more likely to hire you to write about the subject again.

If you play this right, you will be in possession of a burgeoning freelance journalism career: You will have identified your beats. You will have identified your targets—the places where you want to publish the pieces you write. You will have come up with angles on topics that you can pitch. After you publish a piece, you'll have your first clip.

You'll want to make sure that you are not bringing too much academic language into your journalism writing, but a good friend or two can help with that—before you send out your first piece, get some brutal editorial help from friendly readers.

You will need to learn how to pitch articles and interact professionally with editors. Read Kelly J. Baker's 2017 *Chronicle Vitae* article on how to do so, aptly titled "How to Craft a Pitch." You can also hire a writing coach to work with you on your first few pitches and pieces. Your first paying story will likely cover the cost.

Writing books takes a lot of time—years, usually. Writing academic journal articles takes months, sometimes years. Writing short freelance pieces for online venues is fast work, and a great way to balance out longer projects.

Working as a freelance writer is fun, satisfying, hard, creative, and hard. I repeat: It is not easy. There are times when I don't want to do it anymore because it is so very hard. The hard part, usually, has to do with the business, and the money. So let's talk about those things next.

TWENTY-TWO

Run Your Business Like a Business

WHEN I FIRST STARTED FREELANCING FOR MONEY, I ALSO HELD A full-time job at a university. Even though I didn't earn a lot of money freelancing (just a couple thousand dollars a year), I wanted to keep my two income streams separate—my freelancing income stream and my university income stream. So I created a separate business entity for my freelance income.

That was nearly five years ago. Since then, I've left my university position and started freelancing full time. I've published books, freelance articles for magazine, and other writing for money. I also earn money as a writing consultant, as a speaker, and as an editor. Things have really changed since I first started freelancing. And as things have changed and grown, I've had to get better at running my business like a business.

Incorporation

I'm now incorporated. "Pryal Consulting, Inc.," at your service. Let's talk about what lawyers typically call "small business formation." That simply means the various ways that you can organize your business legally. There are lots of ways, but I'll talk about three of them here, the ones that most freelance academics will need to consider.

Required Disclaimer: Although I'm a lawyer, what I'm about to write is not legal advice for you. This information is for informational purposes only. You should contact your attorney to get advice with respect to any particular issue or problem. Remember that laws vary by state.

There are lots of reasons to have a separate company for your freelance business. Because I have a business, I have a business checking account and credit card, and I use those accounts to pay for my business expenses, such as pens, paper, travel expenses, and website hosting. Keeping these expenses in a separate account makes tax time a lot easier. I don't have to mark expenses as business or not, because if I used my business account to pay for them, I know they're business expenses. And as a freelancer, I actually have a ton of little expenses that I'm sure glad I have a separate business card to pay for. Nothing slips through the cracks.

The great thing is, you don't have to incorporate to have a separate checking account or credit card. You only have to have a separate entity with a separate Tax ID from the IRS. In fact, when a freelance academic is just starting out, a sole proprietorship is usually the best idea. A sole proprietorship is a business run by a single person (always a single person), and the business is not registered with the state. You just decide that you are a sole proprietorship, and you are. Then, to get your business's Tax ID number, go the IRS website (at the time of this writing, irs-ein-tax.com), and the process is very straightforward—and instantaneous. You print out the Tax ID, take it to your bank, and open a separate, business checking account.

Another benefit to having a Tax ID is that your personal information is more secure. When I write for magazines—every time—I have to give them a Tax ID for payment. I would hate to hand out my social security number each time. Instead, I give out the Tax ID for my business. You can do the same. Just file for a Tax ID with the IRS, and there you go. If you set up a separate checking account for your payments, all the better—you can deduct your business expenses from your business earnings without any confusion.

One note: If you decide to form a sole proprietorship, you won't get the protections that come with an LLC (a "limited-liability company") or a corporation—namely, protection from liability. Depending on your business, having this protection might be really important. Please consult your lawyer to figure out if an LLC is a better way to go for you. But don't let the need to form an LLC stop you from forming a sole proprietorship now. You can usually convert your sole proprietorship into an LLC when you are ready to do so. Get the benefits of a sole proprietorship now, then figure out if an LLC (or a corporation) are right for you.

Here's what I did. When I began earning freelance income, I formed an LLC right away. Now, forming an LLC costs money: most people have to hire a lawyer to help you with the paperwork. I am a lawyer, so I did my own paperwork. There are also filing fees with your state, and in my state, those are in the hundreds of dollars, annually. Plus, you have to pay your accountant extra to do your LLC's taxes. So be sure that these extra costs are worth the protections an LLC provides.

After a few years, I chose to convert my LLC to a corporation, in particular, an S-Corporation. There are different kinds of corporations, depending on size and other factors. If you are a small business and want the benefits of a corporation without a lot of the hassle, an S-Corporation is your best bet. (Your lawyer can explain why.) There are two main reasons that I chose to convert my LLC to an S-Corp: I save money on my taxes because I can pay myself some of my money in a paycheck, and then some of my money in dividends, which is taxed at a lower rate. And the other reason is because I can have what is called an "Individual 401k," or i401k. (You can only have an i401k if you are the only employee of your corporation.) When I left my academic job, I rolled my institutional retirement plan into my new i401k and then continued to contribute tax-free. There are lots of investment banks that would love to help you set up your i401k for free. But you can only have a corporate-style retirement plan if you have a corporate-style business.

There are drawbacks to having your business structured as a corporation. Your accounting becomes far more complicated. You must pay yourself an actual paycheck; I pay for accounting and payroll software to handle this for me. You must pay corporate payroll taxes too, which are complicated, so you will probably want (or need) to pay for that payroll software. Remember, I'm a lawyer, and I'm good with accounting, and I still pay for that service so I don't have to do all of that figuring. At the time of publication, the cost of that service was approximately forty dollars per month. You will most likely need to pay for an accountant to do your taxes, and your costs there will go up a lot, too. The point is, for as much money as you will save, you will need to figure out how much you will spend. If the savings don't outweigh the expenses and the aggravation, you shouldn't incorporate. Instead, stick with a sole proprietorship, or form an LLC if you need the liability protections.

Bookkeeping, Quoting, and Invoicing

To keep up with my accounting, I use QuickBooks. There is other bookkeeping software out there, including Xero and Freshbooks, and I've tried the others. I like QuickBooks the best. This is not an endorsement, however. As soon as there is bookkeeping software that beats what exists, I will use it. All bookkeeping software is expensive, ungainly, expensive, and expensive. Find the one that works best for you, and use it—even if you don't like it very much.

The short of it is: if you are going to run a business, you need to keep your books.

What I'm talking about here is real bookkeeping, what is called "double-entry" bookkeeping. You don't just want a computer program that will balance your checking account, like Quicken or Mint. You want to keep your books. Research "double-entry bookkeeping" to learn more about it. Basically, if you're spending money, you want to know where that money came from—and so does the IRS. If you spend money on pens, that money has to have come from someplace. Where?

Bookkeeping software keeps track of the money coming in, and of the money going out. That's double-entry, in its most basic sense: every debit (you paying someone) is tied to a credit (someone paying you). If you aren't doing double-entry bookkeeping, then you aren't bookkeeping. You will probably dislike keeping your books, but software like QuickBooks and Xero makes it less painful.

Another feature of bookkeeping software that becomes really important as you start freelancing is invoicing. At the beginning, when you are just starting out and a spreadsheet can keep your books, you can invoice with an email. Later, as you have more business, you will be glad to have invoices incorporated into your bookkeeping software. Using my software, I create invoices, send invoices, and—this is the best part—track my paid and unpaid invoices. At a glance, I can tell who owes me money.

There's plenty of work you will not love to do as a freelancer. I don't enjoy bookkeeping. I don't enjoy invoicing. I don't enjoy quoting jobs. I hate doing tax paperwork. Pretty much, I don't enjoy doing the work that I have to do that keeps my business running like a business. Whenever I'm doing any of those things, because I am me, I complain a lot. Loudly.

My husband eventually gets fed up and yells, "At least you're not grading!"

True. He listened to me moan about grading for 11 years, as I taught college writing, sometimes four sections a semester across multiple campuses across multiple cities. Nothing snaps me back to reality faster than that particular reminder.

That stuff we don't like to do—whether we're reporting to someone else or ourselves—that stuff is called "life." But at least as a freelancer, I really do get to do what I love. Some of the time —most of the time, really. My estimate is that I spend two-thirds of my professional life actually doing the work that I love, and the rest doing tasks that support the work that I love.

And if you think about it, that ratio makes total sense. How many emails with editors do I have to draft before I get a pitch just right? How many invoices do I have to send before a client finally pays me? How many proposals do I have to revise before the client accepts the project—if the client accepts it at all?

You just have to accept this one truth: Even if you are lucky enough that "what you love" is a thing that people will pay you money to do, a lot of the time you will not actually be doing that thing. And that's OK. I've been freelancing full-time for a few years now, and it took me this long to realize that the invoicing, the quoting, the book-balancing are all, in their own way, great work. Because they're my work.

Honestly, I get to do that work in my pajamas, drinking my coffee from my own coffeemaker, on my own couch, with my dog. It's not that bad.

Colleagues—Make Your Own

Another challenge that freelancers face that is less tangible than business formation and bookkeeping but no less daunting is this: Freelancing can be lonely. For a long time, I wondered why people would fork over good money for coworking spaces. Why pay to work with other freelancers when we already pay for places— called houses or apartments—where we can do our work for free?

Then I figured it out. Freelancers may have different motivations for going to coworking spaces, but a primary reason is for the company. I see it when I visit coworking spaces. The freelancers bounce ideas off of each other. They greet each other. They know that someone else knows they're alive. It's a good feeling to know that someone else knows—and cares—that you're alive. When you leave a full-time job to freelance, you lose colleagues. Now, some of you might be thinking: "Awesome. My former colleagues were terrible. I would quit just to get away from being treated like garbage." But the thing is, you probably had one or two colleagues whom you liked. And even the most misanthropic person needs other people to steal ideas from.

But what if you can't afford to pay for a coworking space? If it's people you need, you can of course work in those places called libraries or coffee shops at no (or minimal) charge, but you are unlikely to find many colleagues there who do what you do.

Here's the solution I figured out, quite by accident. I created a network of colleagues, hand-picking people whom I love to bounce ideas off of. But we connect using technology. The people whom I've gathered (and whom I am still gathering) as my colleagues live all over the world. We organize regular monthly videochat meetings. We talk about our career challenges. We figure out how to solve problems we're facing. Usually, when I sign off of these meetings, I have ideas for new articles to pitch or business strategies to implement. They walk away with what they need. In fact, before we say goodbye, we ask each other: "Did you get what you need?" And we always schedule the next meeting before hanging up.

Everyone needs colleagues. But if you are a freelancer, you must create your own circle of colleagues, which is much, much harder—and much, much better. But please, don't try to do it alone. It's too hard. Even if you are an introvert and enjoy being alone, you need colleagues.

Deciding What Jobs to Take

You will, at first, take every job that comes your way. You'll be so excited that people want to pay you to do what you do. And then, after a while, you will realize that you don't have to take every job. This is a strange moment in the life-cycle of a freelancer. It's also an empowering one. The moment you realize you call far more shots than you thought you did.

How do you decide which jobs to take?

My husband majored in physics and economics. (Can you say "major nerd"?) But having him around is great when it comes time to making rational business decisions with my work. He knows all the tricks. And let's just say that I can be a little temperamental sometimes.

Me: "This client is ridiculous! I'm quitting!"

Him: "Your client is ridiculous. You are not quitting."

And he proceeds to explain tactics for how to manage a difficult client relationship. He helps me write strategic emails that help me maintain professional boundaries. Luckily, over the years we've been married, I've managed to absorb a little of his wisdom, so I don't need his intervention 100% of the time. Just sometimes.

One of the favorite terms I've learned from him is "decision matrix." A decision matrix is a super-rational tool for making decisions, allowing you to take a bunch of variables into consideration and keep the seat of your pants out of the equation, so to speak.

When you have a decision to make that has a lot of criteria to consider (literally, a "multi-criteria decision analysis," or MCDA), you use a decision matrix to help you make your decision. I use a decision matrix to help me decide whether I should take on writing, editing, or consulting jobs. I can't be trusted to use my instincts because when it comes to jobs, my instincts aren't trustworthy. Here's why.

Sometimes, I'm presented with work that I feel like I should take because it will help build relationships, or build my résumé, or build my reputation. I call these jobs "3-R" jobs. I feel like I should take the job because a 3-R job, even though it doesn't pay well, might (might!) lead to more work.

Sometimes, I take a job because the money is so good that I feel like I can't say no—even though I'm pretty sure I'll hate the work. After all, I quit an academic job to freelance full time. So there's always a bit of guilt lurking in the back of my mind, telling me that I'm not pulling my weight around the household with the income that I'm generating. (I call these jobs "devil's bargains.")

Sometimes I'm lucky, and I take a job that pays okay, or even well, and I actually enjoy the work, too. (These jobs land in what I call the "sweet spot.")

The thing is, as any good economist (or my husband) will tell you, if you fill up your calendar with 3-R jobs or devil's bargains, then you have no time left for any sweet spot work that might come along. Or, you know, for your next fiction manuscript. The economics term is "opportunity cost": When you choose one alternative, you might get the gains from choosing that alternative, but you lose the potential gains you might have had from the choosing another alternative. If you choose one path, you can't go down the other path.

Given that, as freelancers, we're working with a fixed amount of time, and given that we'd like to make some money, whenever we are presented with time and a project to fill that time with, we need to ask ourselves: "What am I working for?"

Are you working for the money? For the three Rs? Or are you in the sweet spot? You can use a simple decision matrix to help you decide, rationally, which jobs to take—rather than being driven by fears.

My fears, if you look back a few paragraphs, are easy to identify: Is my reputation strong enough? Am I pulling my weight financially?

Start by simply keeping count of the jobs you take. Keep a list —just keep count. Does it feel like you're only taking soul-killing work for the money? Maybe that's because you are. Does it feel like you're taking low-paying work with little reward except to build your reputation? Maybe you're right. Does it feel like you're not having much fun with your work? Maybe that's because you aren't.

Keep track of what you've been doing. Just a simple count. Start counting now. If you can, get some historical data too, to help you. You might be surprised by the results. Count all of your freelance work, everything you've done to earn money or to push your freelance academic career forward even if it didn't pay.

If it turns out you're right, and you have been taking lots of jobs to feed your reputation or your bank account, and not enough to feed your soul, you now have the evidence to prove it. And you can justify saying "no" to a job in the future. You'll know that you're turning a job down because it's time for a different sort of job. You can feel super-rational while you do so, too.

Business Sense

As you can see, you have a lot of choices to make as you prepare to turn your freelance academic work into a business. But you don't have to do all of these things at once. You can start slow. Take one job. Create a spreadsheet to track earnings. Get a Tax ID. Do one thing a week, just one thing. Before you know it, you'll have a career on your hands, one that you love.[1]

TWENTY-THREE

But I'm Still In Higher Ed

IN THE PREVIOUS CHAPTER, "RUN YOUR BUSINESS LIKE A BUSINESS," I talked a lot about business formations and how to turn your freelance academic side-gig into a career.

But what if you still work in higher education in some contingent position or a tenured or tenure-track one? What are the challenges in pursuing freelance academic work if you still count on a paycheck from a college or university?

There is one obvious barrier: departments and institutions may frown on your nonacademic work. They don't want you distracted. They want you to focus on them, naturally. Some institutions have rules that bar you from holding jobs or earning income outside of the institution. When I wrote my first book for money while I was a contingent academic, I was told that some members of my department were worried that my writing would "distract" me from teaching my many sections of composition—even though I was writing a textbook for the very subfield in which I taught.

But there are less obvious barriers as well.

"Megan" (a pseudonym) adjuncts at two different institutions to make ends meet. Despite her multi-campus teaching, she still ends up with a "below-poverty-level adjunct salary." In an interview, she pointed out "one humongous issue" that "has to do with how institutions hire adjuncts and how [adjuncts] are taxed." Megan insists—and I concur—that adjuncts "should be hired as regular freelancers, so that we can actually deduct expenses, such as partial use of home as office, since we are never given an individual office."

Her exasperation is plain in her tone: "It is completely absurd that we are taxed like regular employees, but have absolutely no benefits, and then we cannot even deduct the costs of our own work. This is really too much."

It's true. Freelancers typically lack the security of regular employment, but they have the benefit of deducting lots of expenses: pens, paper, laptops, printers, home office space. Those are all things that adjuncts use to do their jobs.

When you freelance outside the academy, you are doing external work that is not taxed like your work at your institution. The income from that external work is called "1099 income," and you would deduct your freelance expenses against that income. However, finding the time to pursue 1099 income while adjuncting full-time on two campuses can be next to impossible. Most adjuncts are often just too busy.

Would a better solution be to classify adjuncts as 1099 independent contractors rather than as W-2 (full-time) employees? Is such a thing even possible?

To answer my questions, I talked with a tax law professor at the University of North Carolina School of Law, Kathleen DeLaney Thomas. My first question: Under tax law, can adjuncts be classified as 1099 employees?

That's unlikely, according to Thomas. "The IRS has taken the position in most cases that adjunct professors are employees," she said, "and courts have generally agreed." That classification really isn't up to the employer. "In fact," Thomas said, "it can be more expensive for the employer to hire [a W-2] employee because the employer is then responsible for FICA taxes, federal and state unemployment, and possibly worker's comp" whereas employers "can avoid payroll taxes and withholding obligations for independent contractors, who have to pay self-employment taxes on their own."

Because of the benefits that would accrue if they could classify adjuncts as 1099 workers, Thomas explained, "My sense is that schools are classifying their adjuncts as employees to avoid challenge by the IRS."

But what about the classic "freeway flier"—the adjunct who teaches on multiple campuses and lacks almost any institutional support? While "the 'freeway flier' is a sympathetic case," Thomas said, "unfortunately for those professors, the precedent for independent contractor status is not good."

The problem has to do with how courts determine who is an independent contractor and who is a W-2 employee. "The determination," Thomas said, "is generally based on a facts-and-circumstances test, where courts consider a number of factors like how much control the employer exercises, which party invests in work facilities, which party bears the risk of profit or loss, and whether the work is part of the employer's regular business." Most of the factors in that test weigh on the side of the adjunct being a W-2 employee.

She pointed to a United States Tax Court decision, *Schramm v. Commissioner*, T.C. Memo. 2011-212 (Aug. 30, 2011), that "held that an adjunct college professor teaching online courses was an employee, notwithstanding the fact that the professor provided his own computer and Internet connection and had no office at the school." How could that be the case? "Among the factors pointing toward employee status," Thomas said, "were that the school determined the class schedule, managed registration of students, provided the web interface for the class, and bore all risk of profit and loss, along with the fact that the courses taught were part of the school's primary business." Those factors, she said, "are likely to apply to most adjunct professors, even those that work at multiple schools."

In the end—however much adjuncts and other contingent

faculty may feel like they aren't treated as employees—in the eyes of the IRS, they will be for the foreseeable future. Our university teaching will not count as freelance work, which means we won't be able to deduct any expenses related to that work.

I'm sorry to be the bearer of that bad news, but Megan's question was an important one. Those of us who embrace the freelancer ethos need to understand the structural limitations on our freelancing work.

But we can still find freelancing work outside of our institutions. The university is, after all, just another client (as I explain in Chapter 10). So you want to deduct your laptop, pens, printer, paper, and all of you other purchases on your taxes? Great —you can. Earn some money through your freelancing work. If you can, turn down that fourth or fifth adjunct course, and use that time to earn money through actual freelance work instead. Educate yourself about IRS rules. It's not that complicated, I promise, and there are great resources out there. The Freelancers Union has lots of them online.

I know that everything I've recommended requires risk-taking on your part. I've taken those risks, too, and they're scary. One day, I walked away from relatively secure employment—as secure as a non-tenure-track faculty member can get, really. I walked away because the working conditions were just too hard. That was one of the scariest days of my life. I didn't know how we were going to keep our house. I'd written a plan of how we were going to live on one salary, and the plan was severe.

But then this magical thing happened. Although the first year was a little lean, I started making money. I had all of this time to try new things, and some of those things started to pan out. I realized that no one knows how to rustle up work like a person who taught first-year writing on multiple campuses in multiple cities while pregnant. I just needed to redirect that energy in a way that benefited a career that I controlled, rather than benefiting institutions that didn't care about me at all. Oh, and I needed to take it easier on myself, too.

You can do it too. You can take all of your energy and drive and succeed in whatever path you choose, whether that path is remaining in academia and freelancing on the side, or working part-time in academia and part-time freelancing, or leaving academia completely like I did and finding an entirely new career that makes you happier, healthier, and more successful—however you define success.[1]

TWENTY-FOUR

It's Not Personal. It's Strictly Business.

RECENTLY, I WAS TALKING WITH A FELLOW FREELANCE academic about some of the challenges we've faced making the transition out of academia and into freelancing. We both pointed to a similar challenge: A lot of the work that we were expected to do for free in the academy is work that we charge money for now.

That may not sound like a challenge at first mention. Actually, if you are still in the academy, the notion of getting paid actual money for some of the "bonus work" that you do might sound outstanding. Indeed, as my friend and I agreed, freelance academics can sometimes manage to pay the bills when we are able to effectively charge money for our hard work as editors, writing coaches, and the like.

But getting paid as a freelancer for work that you used to do for free as a faculty member can get tricky.

Here's an example. When I was in the academy, I often edited articles for colleagues and helped them with their other writing projects. I'm a good editor. In fact, I'm a trained editor who worked at newspapers and PR departments back before graduate school. I have a master's degree in nonfiction writing in addition to my doctorate. I coached people through writing challenges for work before entering the academy. When I became a faculty member, doing the same editing work for colleagues came naturally to me.

What I began to notice, however, was that those colleagues rarely returned the favor. Perhaps they felt that they didn't have the writing chops to assist me with my work. Or perhaps they just didn't view my research and writing as important. I was non-tenure-track, after all, and my research didn't count toward promotion and retention. Helping me with my writing just wasn't as urgent.

Whatever the reason, I did a lot of uncompensated work as a writing coach and editor when I was in the academy. I considered it service to my departments. Then I left the academy, and one of my income streams became writing coaching and editing—not just for academics, but for novelists, journalists, and more. This time, when academic colleagues came to me for the same kind of writing help that I used to give them for free, I asked them to pay me for my time and expertise. Some of them dipped into their research funds and did so.

Some of them got mad.

My friend and fellow freelance academic reported the same sort of anger and annoyance from her former colleagues as well.

So what gives? If you're a freelancer and former academic, a lot of these business challenges arise because the relationships you have—or used to have—are with people still in the academy. Some of them, frankly, do not want to pay you for services you used to provide them for free. How do you manage the emotions of your former colleagues? How do you handle friends (or "friends") who come to you for help and want that help for free? How can you tell if someone is a friend or a client?

Here are some rules of thumb to keep in mind when embarking on a freelance academic career, rules that will help you transition your relationships as you transition your career out of the academy. First, remember what Michael Corleone said in The Godfather:

It's not personal. It's strictly business.

Business Etiquette Is Crucial

A lot of the confusion in business relationships between people who are also friends arises because the participants don't practice proper business etiquette. Instead, they think that because they are friends they can ignore business etiquette. But actually, the opposite is true. When friends do business together, business etiquette becomes even more important.

Here are two very different examples that show why this is true.

Example 1: I have friends who own a magazine. I always pay for my subscription. But they have other friends who expect free subscriptions simply because they know the magazine's publishers. The thing is, my publisher-friends make a living—feed their children—from this magazine. Why would any so-called friend pass up the chance to pay them for their hard work? Asking for a free subscription is not friendship, it's mooching. And moochers, dear readers, are the worst.

Example 2: I have friends who own a restaurant. I love to eat there. I buy delicious food and wine, and I always tip the waitstaff ridiculously well. I never, ever mention that I'm friends with the owners. Name-dropping the owners of a restaurant is not only annoying to everyone who works in the restaurant, it's pretentious, too. Ugh. But the owners have other so-called friends who come in to eat and expect special treatment—free drinks, free desserts, all sorts of things. They wave their "friendship" around like a discount coupon, mooching right and left.

To preserve your friendship with someone you would also like to do business with, you must do your utmost to behave in a professional manner. If you are the client, then pay for your friend's services in full, in a timely fashion. That's it. Period. You don't get a discount unless your friend offers one. Don't even ask. If you ask, you are a moocher. Worse, you risk losing your friend forever.

If you are the freelancer selling your services, you also must behave with proper business etiquette. Here's what that means: Don't get aggravated with your friend/client over personal issues. Keep your personal knowledge of your client out of your business relationship. I know from experience that sometimes, keeping things professional can be really hard. Sometimes you want to get annoyed with your client. Sometimes you feel like it would be easier to take things personally. But trust me, once you realize that "it's strictly business," a weight lifts from your shoulders.

Michael Corleone was right. (About this at least—he's not a model dude otherwise.)

Here's an example from my own freelance academic career: I had a client who paid me monthly with a personal check. (Others usually pay me via credit card or PayPal.) Often, she was late with her payments, but I overlooked that behavior, attributing it to her slightly scatterbrained nature. Then one month, she bounced a check. I had literally never had a client bounce a check before. Not only did I not have my fee from her that month, the bank charged a bounced check fee. Depending on your bank, those run around twenty dollars. (These fees are called "nonsufficient funds fees" or NSF fees.) I was super pissed off when the check bounced. But I talked with some other small business owners and got some good advice. "It's just business, Katie," they said. "Put an NSF policy on your invoices from now on." What about the client? "Charge her a fee, and send the invoice again."

So I did. And the client paid it, not only with no questions asked, but gratefully and apologetically. And I felt an immense relief. I didn't need to feel strong emotions. I just needed to run my business. The next time she bounced a check (yes, it happened again), I didn't even flinch. I just did the paperwork. Bounced checks, like clients, are part of a freelancer's life. She's not a bad person. She's just a client who makes mistakes—ones that I don't take personally—because they're not personal.

Who Is a Friend?

But how do you know who is a client in the first place? What about those friends who think the work you do for them should be free? The rule is simple:

A friend can return a favor. A client's favor is money.

This rule is hard to follow when you first leave the academy. At first, you don't know what favors you need. You don't know anything, let alone what to charge your clients. You hardly know what kind of paper you need for your printer. But as you go along, you start to figure out how to distinguish clients from friends. Friends do things for one another. Clients take the things you do for them, and they give you money in return.

The transactions are different.

But notice—and notice well—that they are both transactions. Friends still make a trade. They just trade favors. My friends and I refer to these favors as "chits." (A chit, by the dictionary, refers to a voucher that records a sum owed to someone else.)

Because I'm a writing coach, discerning a friend or acquaintance from client can be tricky. Other writers send me emails asking to "pick my brain" about my career path and my writing. I tend to err on the side of not-client, so I end up with a lot of hours spent doing writing and career coaching for free, for people who have no intention of doing anything for me in return. They either don't want to—because they don't understand the system of chits—or they can't—because they don't have the connections or know-how to provide anything in return.

I actually believe that most, if not all, people in the situation I just described can indeed provide something in return. The problem is that many people don't understand chits. You, dear reader, are going to understand chits.

Here's how chits work: if you ask someone to do you a professional favor, offer to do them something in return. Think of something specific that you might be able to do for them, like this: "Thank you for your time today. I'm an excellent copyeditor. If you ever need copyediting in the future, I'll be happy to copyedit an article for you." The other person might not realize that you have that expertise. The best thing about offering a valuable chit in return is that you make yourself a valuable part of the person's network—rather than a moocher.

It follows, too, that if you are the person providing a service, you can tell your friend what you would like in return as your chit. You can't expect someone to read your mind and know what you need. Here's how I recently handled this very situation. I met a new freelancer for the first time just a couple of a weeks ago. Prior to our meeting, we knew each other casually, mostly from social media. She initiated the meeting. Just before our meeting, I scoped out her website and studied her expertise. Now, I already knew why she wanted to talk to me because she'd told me in an email—I knew what she was getting from me. What could she give me in return? At the beginning of our meeting, I told her exactly what I wanted as my chit, something that I knew she would be happy to give to me in return. Suddenly, our relationship was in professional balance.

Because that's the thing about chits. When you find yourself able to do return favor to someone who has helped you, you feel good about yourself. You feel that you aren't a mooch. You feel like you're pulling your professional weight, which is a great feeling. By handing my new friend the opportunity to give me something in return in the future, I put us on equal footing. I did it on purpose because I wanted to be friends with this person. I wanted her to know that I respect her professionally.

But not every client is a friend. If you're still in the academy, and we weren't friends before I left, and you ask me to edit your new article, I will ask you to pay me for my time and expertise. We weren't colleagues then, and we aren't colleagues now. Furthermore, I don't have a service requirement to meet. (Hell, as a contingent faculty member, I never did, I was just afraid of getting fired, so I did all I could to ingratiate myself.)

These days I'm a freelancer with whom you are asking to

161

consult because you feel like you need extra help. That's great. Furthermore, you are asking me to do a job that is squarely within the defined parameters of the work I get paid to do. You only have to read my website to know that. Indeed, you probably already know that. You already know that I'm a great editor because you likely have had me edit your stuff before, back when we were colleagues. But things are different now. Now I edit for money. That might seem crazy to you because you still draw a salary from a university. But it's true. I make a living helping academics and other writers make their writing better. And my time is valuable.

It's not personal. It's strictly business.[1]

TWENTY-FIVE

Three Stories from Freelance Academics

I'VE SPENT THE LAST FEW CHAPTERS TALKING ABOUT HOW I DO THINGS as a freelance academic. But what about others? I thought I'd add a few more voices to the mix. How are others faring after leaving the academy? Are they succeeding?

For answers, I reached out to three freelance academics who are doing just that. Heidi Giusto, Greer McPhaden, and Jennifer Polk are all post-academics who have successfully transitioned into freelance work. Their stories can help you, directly or indirectly, succeed as freelance academics. Heidi, Greer, and Jennifer are from different places (Durham, NC; New York, NY; and Toronto, Canada). They have had different training and different paths through the academy. But they share a common quality: They've all made their way as self-employed freelancers and entrepreneurs.

I posed the same three questions to each of them: What was the hardest thing for you when you transitioned out of the academy? What's the most important gift you've given yourself? What advice do you have for new freelance academics? Here's what they had to say.

Freelance Academic No. 1: Heidi Scott Giusto

About Heidi: A White woman living in Raleigh, NC
Degree: Ph.D. in history
Former life: Graduate student, writing center tutor at a large university
Currently: Consultant, writer, editor, and owner of Career Path Writing Solutions (careerpathwritingsolutions.com)

What was the hardest thing for you when you transitioned out of the academy?

Heidi writes, "My immediate transition was not that difficult because I had been preparing for quite some time." But, she notes: "As my business has grown—I'm approaching the two-year mark for running Career Path Writing Solutions—I've become aware of my lack of formal business training." In retrospect, she says, "If I could do it all over again, I would have researched whether I could have taken some business courses while I was [at my former institution]."

What has been the most important gift you've given yourself as you've made your way as a freelancer?

Choosing a fulfilling career was Heidi's gift to herself. She enjoys "feeling like I'm making a difference in people's lives in a direct way. Because I help with a variety of high-stakes documents ranging from résumés, cover letters, and LinkedIn profiles, to graduate school personal statements to website content to college applications, I get to help people at various, key moments of their lives." Heidi's words show how much she loves what she does: "To ease a person's anxiety level and burden when undergoing such stressful moments is gratifying. My job is very fulfilling."

What advice do you have for new freelance academics?

"First, take time to brainstorm and determine your niche," she said. "I recommend choosing a field or area you already enjoy." Second, "Start getting experience and building your network outside of academia sooner rather than later. It takes a while to build a strong referral network, but once that takes shape, business snowballs." Third, and on a related note, "Don't let fear paralyze you. People self-impose limitations that lead to inaction because they fear failure, so don't let any insecurities weigh you down." In short: Figure out your strengths, build your network right away, and believe in yourself.

————

Freelance Academic No. 2: Greer McPhaden

About Greer: A Black woman living in New York, NY
Degree: M.B.A.
Former life: Director of research operations at a university medical center
Currently: Consultant, writer, and owner at 272 Words (272words.net).

What was the hardest thing for you when you transitioned out of the academy?

Not having anyone to talk to about her choice to leave academia and start a business was the hardest thing, Greer said. "Academics and even academic administrators aren't entrepreneurs," she told me. "Provided you've chosen the right field of study, [academia is] not a risky path. Risk makes people uncomfortable." Many of her colleagues found it hard to relate to her risky choice to leave the academy. But she understood why: "Just deciding to start a company...is a very risky thing when you have a whole academic path in front of you. It's hard for people to be supportive of your made-up job when you've had a steady job at a top university for over a decade."

What has been the most important gift you've given yourself as you've made your way as a freelancer?
Becoming a freelance entrepreneur in the first place—"realizing that I'm okay with this"—was her greatest gift to herself. "I didn't know I was this person," she said. "I like order, and I assumed that meant I needed to know where I'm going to be, and what I'm going to be doing, 12 months from now." And yet, she told me, "it's been over 18 months and I'm still alive. I live in my same apartment. I'm not living on ramen noodles. And most people think I look more relaxed. It took about a year to come to this conclusion, but now that I have, I'm going with it."

What advice do you have for new freelance academics?
Like Heidi, Greer was very clear with her advice: "Get a coach, a mastermind group, or a meet-up group. If you are the only person in your head every day, you will go crazy." She learned first-hand from her own experience of feeling isolated: "You—and most of the people you know—only know one way of living and working. You will compare everything to that"; that is, to academia. Instead, "you need someone who will cheer you on and tell you that what you are going through is normal."

———

FREELANCE ACADEMIC NO. 3: JENNIFER POLK

About Jennifer: A White woman living in Toronto, Canada
Degree: Ph.D. in history
Former life: Graduate student, frustrated freelance researcher, and virtual assistant
Currently: Coach, speaker, consultant, and owner at From Ph.D.

to Life (fromphdtolife.com) and cofounder of Beyond the
Professoriate (beyondprof.com).

**What was the hardest thing for you when you transitioned out
of the academy?**
Jennifer felt "very alone" when she first left the academy.
"Everyone I knew who shared my educational background was
either working as a professor or trying hard to do so." She added,
"Even my freelance clients were convinced I'd end up a professor."
And she didn't feel like she had anyone to turn to for help: "No
one had any other ideas for me, not really." So she hired someone
to help her and reached out to others: "It was only after I hired a
career coach and started to do informational interviews with
fellow Ph.D.'s who'd moved on to other careers—and then getting
on Twitter and seeking out people with my same interests and
concerns—that I felt better able to take positive steps forward."

**What has been the most important gift you've given yourself as
you've made your way as a freelancer?**
"Patience," Jennifer told me. Although she says she has to be
careful to guard against "complacency," Jennifer noted that
"patience more often is about giving myself the time and space
and compassion to follow my own path, whatever it is."

What advice do you have for new freelance academics?
First, Jennifer urges us to consider identity a malleable thing:
"Your degree or research area or award-winning syllabi are not
who you are. Who you are isn't tied to any one job that you do,
such as working as a professor." She deliberately used the phrase
"working as" rather than "being a" professor—because "language
matters." Second, Jennifer told me, "If you're feeling uncertain or
unmoored as I once did (and still do on occasion!), connect with
your roots...that is, your priorities, goals, values, and character
strengths—and then act in accordance with them."

All three of these freelance academics took different paths and now do very different work. But their stories share common threads, and common advice: Find your community. Don't be afraid to ask for help. Figure out what you're good at and what you love, and then do it. Believe in yourself.[1]

TWENTY-SIX

Finding Stability as a Freelance Academic

WHEN I STARTED WRITING ABOUT BEING A FREELANCE ACADEMIC FIVE years ago, I was a Ph.D. on leave from my contingent faculty job —trying to figure out how to find a fulfilling career in a higher-education system that did not value my work. The solution, I ultimately decided, was to value myself, leave higher education, and create work that I liked.

Skip forward from 2014 to now, and I've left academe, started my freelancing business, and created a relatively stable life for myself doing work that I (usually) enjoy. But the key word in that sentence is "stable." Too many Ph.D.s-turned-freelancers have trouble finding stability, especially now that more and more work across all fields is outsourced from full-time positions to what has been dubbed the "gig economy." (I write more about the gig economy in Chapter 19, "How to Start Working for Yourself.") Those of us living from job to job know that freelancing can give your nerves a drubbing. I, for one, didn't leave the stress of a contingent job to live an even more unstable life. Here's how I found stability as a freelance academic.

Put Safeties in Place

For me, at least, the news cycle has been exhausting ever since 2016. Every day, it seems, there's a new horrifying thing. Just living through it has been hard. I know that others feel the same.

As a freelance journalist, though, the news cycle has been a particular kind of wrecking ball. I'm someone who is paid to write about those horrifying things, and I'm beginning to hate that particular slice of my freelance work. It's hard to write in-depth coverage of an event when, 24 hours later, my work might well be out of date. And when I try to write a story that keeps up with the news cycle, it's even more exhausting than usual. Everything else I'm working on (not to mention my private life) must be put on hold to write it. Before the current administration and its incessant horror, a quick turnaround on a reported piece might be three or four days. Now? The turnaround time is twenty-four hours at most, and even then the magazine might kill your story because something more atrocious has happened in the meantime.

And that's just my freelance journalism work. There's also the rest of my career that I cobble together through freelance consulting, editing, and more. I never know how much money will come in each month, and when I'll strike it big—relatively speaking. Basically, working as a freelancer can be exhausting because it can feel like you're always on a financial roller-coaster. The freedom and flexibility are huge pluses, but the sheer unpredictability of it can wear you out.

I've learned how to put safeties in place to create a more stable life as a freelancer. Stability is not just about bringing in a consistent income. It's also about generating consistent work and creating a community I can count on. Those three things— consistent money, work, and community—are the three legs of the table I'm building my freelance career on now. Whether you are an academic thinking about starting a side business, or you are leaving higher education entirely, here are some things to consider about each of those legs.

Stable, Consistent Money

It is a truism of freelancing that getting paid is hard. Our clients often sit on our money. Just because you've done the work doesn't mean that you'll have your money. So it is your job to ensure that you have money and aren't, therefore, at the mercy of clients who can't or won't pay you on time.

Here's a small trick I learned from my friend, mentor, and writer, Claire McGuire. It was some of the best freelancing advice I've ever received: Pay yourself a paycheck each month. Keep the amount consistent, and keep it within your means.

This trick requires having two checking accounts. One is your business account. This is the account where the income from your clients goes—and from which you draw your regular paycheck. The other account is your personal account, and that's where you deposit your paycheck. Write yourself a paycheck each month (or just do a transfer, if the accounts are in the same bank). Make sure the amount is the same every month and always well within your means.

If you follow these rules, you will have a predictable income. You will always know how much you will "make" each month. Even though the amount in your business account might fluctuate, your paycheck stays the same. One month you might make a lot. But the next month you might make less. That's okay. Your paycheck is stable. In Chapter 22, "Run Your Business Like a Business," I describe how to set up business checking accounts and other business details. Be sure to read that chapter before you start your business.

When I was first getting started as a freelancer, my monthly paycheck amount was low. That's because what I had in the bank was low, and I didn't know what to expect in the future. I had no financial cushion. Now that I've been doing this for a while, the monthly paycheck amount has grown—slightly. I can look at what I have in the bank and project forward as I give myself a steady paycheck.

Honestly, a steady paycheck, no matter how small, is something that every freelancer dreams of—or at least this freelancer does. As you find stability as a freelance academic, get off the income roller-coaster as quickly as you can.

Stable, Consistent Work

Finding consistent work is the hobgoblin of all freelancers. A caveat: none of the following ideas will be perfect for every reader —mostly they apply to someone like me who is a writer and editor. But hopefully the concepts will work for you in whatever self-employment you are pursuing.

When I first started freelance writing, I got some good advice from a writer friend: once you've pitched an idea and written for a magazine, she said, you pitch a series next. In other words, take the one stand-alone piece of work and turn it into predictable, consistent work. Take a one-off and create a steady income stream.

At the beginning of my freelance career, I did that twice. I wrote a single piece, then on the basis of that single piece, pitched the editor a column. Both times, the editor said yes. With those yeses, I had my first steady, predictable work. The lesson I learned there was this: whenever I write for a magazine, and the editors seem to like what I've produced, I pitch a continuing column on the subject. Often they say no, but sometimes they say yes. Sometimes they just buy the sample pitches I suggest, or they keep me on tap as a go-to person for a certain beat. But those things are good outcomes, too.

To look at this in a bigger-picture fashion, the idea here is to standardize the services you offer—whether they are editing services, technical skills you learned in graduate school, or some independent skill you pursued on your own. What I mean is this: don't just do piecemeal work for piecemeal clients. You don't want to be cold-pitching all the time, because that requires doing two tasks: building trust with a new client as well as selling your services. Finding a way to turn the first job you do for a client into a continuing source of paid work cuts out the first task (building trust) and lets you skip straight to the second.

Two final notes about building consistent work.

First, if you do successful work for clients, ask them for two things in return: a testimonial (have them email it to you so you have it in writing) and referrals. Put the testimonial on your website and on whatever social media you use, such as a Google Business or Facebook Business page.

Second, always have a clean, up-to-date résumé ready as a safety net. Sometimes you need to bow out of freelancing for a while, and there's nothing wrong with that.

Stable, Consistent Community

I knew, of course, that freelance work meant going it alone, but I was nonetheless surprised by just how lonely this sort of work can be. I spend so much of my time alone—even more than was the case in graduate school or when I was teaching. I'm fortunate, however. I stumbled, very much by accident, into a virtual and long-distance community of like-minded freelancers.

While I found my community of freelancer colleagues by accident, maintaining those relationships is something I do very deliberately. I try to schedule Skype and phone chats after I meet people via social media, and work hard not to let the connections lapse. I keep a calendar and ensure that I stay in touch with my fellow freelancers regularly. Indeed, I call them "colleagues," because that is what they are. Although I don't go to work at an office or a department, they are colleagues with whom I share my career failures and successes and upon whom I depend for support. I look out for them, and they look out for me. The stability of that community is the heart of my freelancing career.

Five years after starting on the path of a freelance academic, I've managed to create a career I can (mostly) count on, which, in the grand scheme of things, is all I could wish for.

I wish the same for you.[1]

Recommended Reading and Resources

Here is a list of books and websites, in alphabetical order, that I recommend you take a look at if you need more help as you transition from full-time academic to freelance academic.

I'm certain that I've forgotten some, and there are more being created all the time. Friends: If I have forgotten your book or website, or if you have one to recommend for an updated edition of this book, please email it to me at contact@krgp.ink.

Kelly J. Baker, *Grace Period: A Memoir in Pieces*, Snowraven Books, 2017.

Kelly J. Baker, *Sexism Ed: Essays on Gender and Labor in Academia*, Snowraven Books, 2018.

Kelly J. Baker et al., *Succeeding Outside the Academy: Career Paths beyond the Humanities, Social Sciences, and STEM*, University Press of Kansas, 2018.

Susan Basalla et al., *"So What Are You Going to Do with That?": Finding Careers Outside Academia* (Third Edition), University of Chicago Press, 2014.

Beyond the Professoriate, beyondprof.com, created by Jennifer Polk and Maren Wood.

Marc Bousquet, *How the University Works: Higher Education and the Low-Wage Nation*, NYU Press, 2008.

Tressie McMillan Cottom, *Lower Ed: The Troubling Rise of For-Profit Colleges in the New Economy*, The New Press, 2018.

Roger Fisher et al., *Getting to Yes: Negotiating Agreement Without Giving In* (Updated, Revised Edition), Penguin, 2011.

The Freelancer's Union, freelancersunion.org. From their About Us page: "The largest and fast-growing organization representing the 57 million independent workers across the country. We give our 375,000+ members a powerful voice through policy advocacy, benefits, and community."

Karen Kelsky, *The Professor Is In: The Essential Guide To Turning Your Ph.D. Into a Job*, Random House, 2015.

Sarah Kendzior, *The View from Flyover Country: Dispatches from the Forgotten America*, Flatiron Books, 2018.

Patricia A. Matthew, *Written/Unwritten: Diversity and the Hidden Truths of Tenure*, The University of North Carolina Press, 2016.

Lisa Munro, lisamunro.net, writing coach and alternative career coaching.

M.R. Nelson, *Navigating the Path to Industry: A Hiring Manager's Advice for Academics Looking for a Job in Industry*, Annorlunda Books, 2014.

Catherine J. Prendergast, *Buying into English: Language and*

Investment in the New Capitalist World, University of Pittsburgh Press, 2008.

Alexandrea J. Ravenelle, *Hustle and Gig: Struggling and Surviving in the Sharing Economy,* University of California Press, 2019.

Melanie V. Sinche, *Next Gen PhD: A Guide to Career Paths in Science,* Harvard University Press, 2016.

Miya Tokumitsu, *Do What You Love: And Other Lies About Success & Happiness,* Regan Arts., 2015.

Jennifer Brown Urban et al., *Building a Career Outside Academia: A Guide for Doctoral Students in the Behavioral and Social Sciences,* American Psychological Association, 2018.

Who Pays Writers? whopayswriters.com. From the WPW About page: *Who Pays Writers?* is an anonymous, crowd-sourced list of which publications pay freelance writers—and how much.

Notes

Prologue: A Lecturer's Almanac

1. An earlier version of this chapter first appeared as an essay in *Hybrid Pedagogy* in October of 2013.

Introduction: A Manifesto for the Freelance Academic

1. Rebecca Shuman, *The Chronicle of Higher Education*, "Hanging Up on a Calling," (Jan. 27, 2014), Jacqui Shine, *Chronicle Vitae*, "Love and Other Secondhand Emotions" (Feb. 3, 2014), William Pannapacker, *The Chronicle of Higher Education*, "On Graduate School and 'Love'" (Oct. 1, 2013).
2. Portions of this chapter first appeared as an essay in *Chronicle Vitae* in October of 2014.

3. On Writing

1. Sarah Kendzior, "What's the Point of Academic Publishing," *Chronicle Vitae*, January 24, 2014.
2. Portions of this chapter first appeared as an essay in *Chronicle Vitae* in August of 2015.

5. Negative Capability

1. To get the full picture, read what is colloquially called The Wainstein Report. You can find it by Googling "The Wainstein Report." The full title is, "Investigation of Irregular Classes in the Department of African and Afro-American Studies at the University of North Carolina at Chapel Hill," Kenneth L. Wainstein et al., October 16, 2014.

6. Losing My Affiliation

1. Portions of this chapter first appeared as an essay in *Chronicle Vitae* in March of 2015.

8. Bridging Academia

1. Portions of this chapter first appeared as an essay in *Chronicle Vitae* in March of 2017.

9. Quit Lit Is About Labor Conditions

1. Leonard Cassuto, "The Grief of the Ex-Academic," *The Chronicle of Higher Education*, Feb. 25, 2018. Sarah Brown, "She Wrote a Farewell Letter to Colleagues. Then 80,000 People Read It," *The Chronicle of Higher Education*, Feb. 15, 2018.
2. Portions of this chapter first appeared as an essay in *Women in Higher Education* in June of 2018.

10. The University Is Just Another Client

1. Portions of this chapter first appeared as an essay in *Chronicle Vitae* in February of 2015.

14. What's Your BATNA?

1. Portions of this chapter first appeared as an essay in *Chronicle Vitae* in November of 2015.

15. Leaving a Legacy Off the Tenure Track

1. Harry F. Harlow et al., "Learning Motivated by a Manipulation Drive," *Journal of Experimental Psychology*, Vol. 40.2, April 1950, 228-234.
2. Edward L. Deci, "Effects of Externally Mediated Rewards on Intrinsic Motivation," *Journal of Personality and Social Psychology*, 18.1, 1971, 105-115.
3. Portions of this chapter first appeared as an essay in *Chronicle Vitae* in March of 2016.

16. Why Attend Conferences as a Freelance Academic?

1. Portions of this chapter first appeared as an essay in *Chronicle Vitae* in October of 2016.

Notes

17. Why Am I Teaching Again?

1. Portions of this chapter first appeared as an essay in *Chronicle Vitae* in August of 2016.

19. How to Start Working for Yourself

1. Portions of this chapter first appeared as an essay in *Chronicle Vitae* on July 14, 2016.

21. So You Want to Be a Freelance Writer

1. Jennifer Polk, *University Affairs* (Canada), "Instead of trying to satisfy all of your interests with one job, consider compartmentalizing," April 10, 2017.

22. Run Your Business Like a Business

1. Portions of this chapter first appeared in essays in *The Huffington Post* in July of 2015, in *Chronicle Vitae* in July of 2015, and in *Chronicle Vitae* in July of 2016.

23. But I'm Still In Higher Ed

1. Portions of this chapter first appeared as an essay in *Chronicle Vitae* in July of 2015.

24. It's Not Personal. It's Strictly Business.

1. Portions of this chapter first appeared as an essay in *Chronicle Vitae* in December of 2015.

25. Three Stories from Freelance Academics

1. An earlier version of this chapter first appeared as an essay in *Chronicle Vitae* in May of 2015.

26. Finding Stability as a Freelance Academic

1. An earlier version of this chapter first appeared as an essay in the *Chronicle of Higher Education* in September of 2017.

Acknowledgments

Many people help make a book possible, and the same is true for this book, but perhaps even more true for this book. A freelancer is only a strong as the community who supports her, and I owe everything to mine.

I owe ideas to Sara Littlejohn, Brandy Grabow Brown, Greer McPhaden, Catherine Prendergast, and Tonya Ritola, my colleagues and friends who have sustained me through the years. Alexa Chew and Kelly J. Baker, in particular, have stood close when I needed support most.

I owe my coauthors Ruth McKinney, Jordynn Jack, and Alexa Chew, who have created books with me, which is an unbelievable feat, one that creates a relationship that lasts forever.

I owe my local community in Chapel Hill, including my favorite place to write, La Vita Dolce cafe, its owner Annie, and its manager Erin, who have always welcomed me. And now my local community includes so much of my family as well: my sister and her family, my aunts and uncles, and even my parents. I'm so glad we're all within shouting distance.

I owe my early mentors, Claire McGuire, Ann Garvin, and Gabriela Montell, without whom I wouldn't be writing this book at all.

I owe the group I found as I first made my way as a freelance academic, who were always supportive and giving, in no particular order: Elizabeth Keenan, Rebecca Schuman, Liana M. Silva, Annemarie Pérez, Jen Polk, Heidi Giusto, Lisa Munro, Lee Skallerup-Bessette, and Sarah Kendzior. I'm sure I'm forgetting a few of you, and I'm sorry.

I owe the Tall Poppy Writers, my women writers collective, who have supported me through the years, including the years of this transition from professor to writer. Ann Garvin, Camille Pagán, Kelly Harms, Amy Impellizzeri, Sonja Yoerg, Sandra Block, Amy Sue Nathan, Kelly Simmons, Susan Gloss, Janie Chang, and the rest of you amazing women—I'm so glad I can count on you.

I owe Lauren Faulkenberry, my partner in this incredible business of writing and publishing—I wouldn't do it any other way.

And, as always, I thank my two children and my husband, who inspire me constantly.

About the Author

Katie Rose Guest Pryal is a novelist, journalist, essayist, and former law professor. She is the author of the Hollywood Lights novels, which include *Entanglement, Chasing Chaos,* and *Fallout Girl,* and many works of nonfiction, which include *Life of the Mind Interrupted: Essays on Mental Health and Disability in Higher Education* and *The Freelance Academic: Transform Your Creative Life and Career.*

As a journalist and essayist, her work has appeared in *Catapult, Women in Higher Education, The Toast, Dame Magazine, The Chronicle of Higher Education, Motherwell,* and more. She is a member of the Tall Poppy Writers (tallpoppies.org), a collective of women authors who support one another and connect with readers. Visit her website and blog at katieroseguestpryal.com, and stay in touch with her via her email letter, pryalnews.com.

f facebook.com/krgpryal

y twitter.com/krgpryal

O instagram.com/krgpryal

a amazon.com/author/krgp

BB bookbub.com/authors/katie-rose-guest-pryal

g goodreads.com/krgpryal